Injia on Statutory Interpretation in Papua New Guinea and the Pacific

Salamo Injia

University of Papua New Guinea Press and Bookshop, 2013

Injia on Statutory Interpretation in Papua New Guinea and the Pacific

ISBN: 978-9980-87-901-1

PUBLISHED BY:
The University of Papua New Guinea Press and Bookshop
PO Box 413
University PO, NCD
Papua New Guinea
Email: upngpress@gmail.com

FOREWORD

This textbook is one of eight (8) textbooks written under my hand and supervision:

'Injia on Criminal Offences in Papua New Guinea and the Pacific'

'Injia on Criminal Practice and Procedure in Papua New Guinea and the Pacific'

'Injia on Sentencing in Papua New Guinea and the Pacific'

'Injia on Statutory Interpretation in Papua New Guinea and the Pacific'

'Injia on Coronial Proceedings in Papua New Guinea and the Pacific'

'Injia on Investigatory Practice in Papua New Guinea and the Pacific'

'Injia on Contempt of Court in Papua New Guinea and the Pacific'

'Injia on Evidence in Papua New Guinea and the Pacific'

Each of those textbooks is an effort to offer to Judicial officers, legal practitioners and students of law a comprehensive set of principles and practical guidelines on criminal law and practice in Papua New Guinea and the Pacific. The work undertaken under the auspices of AusAID through the PNG-Australia Law and Justice Partnership Project is an extension of a similar project undertaken previously in writing the textbook *Criminal Law and Practice in Papua New Guinea* co-authored by myself, Professor Don Chalmers, Dr Weisbrot and Justice Andrew.

The textbooks will be of great benefit to the criminal justice system in Papua New Guinea and the Pacific and specifically will assist judges, magistrates, lawyers, law students and police officers in the performance of their duties.

The assistance of AusAID and its development practitioner Mr Errol Gibson who provided research and spent countless hours in the production of these textbooks is acknowledged.

Sir Salamo Injia, Kt

Chief Justice of Papua New Guinea

22nd September 2013

TABLE OF CONTENTS

TABLE OF CONTENTS

TABLE OF CONTENTS

TABLE OF CONTENTS

INTRODUCTION

It is business of the legislature to make the law through statutes, and it is business of the Courts to interpret them.[1]

In the interpretation of any statutory provision the starting point must inevitably be the *Constitution of the Independent State of Papua New Guinea* and the Organic Laws because:

- those constitutional laws are the supreme law of Papua New Guinea[2];

  and

- a law inconsistent with it is, to the extent of the inconsistency, invalid and ineffective[3], unless the Act specifically provides otherwise[4].

Whilst the National Parliament is the supreme law-making body, its law-making power is therefore still subject to section 11 the *Constitution of the Independent State of Papua New Guinea.*[5]

Section 10 of the *Constitution of the Independent State of Papua New Guinea* states:

> 'All written laws (other than this Constitution) shall be read and construed subject to --
>
> (a) in any case – this Constitution; and
>
> (b) in the case of Acts of Parliament – any relevant organic laws; and
>
> (c) in the case of adopted laws or subordinate legislative enactments -- the organic laws and the laws by or under which they are enacted or made,

---

[1] See Blackstone, 'Commentaries on the Laws of England', 1765, Volume 1, page 87.

Refer also to: Speech by The Honorable Justice Susan Crennan AC, Justice of the High Court of Australia, 'Blackstone's "signs" and statutory interpretation', Victoria Bar Continuing Legal Education Lecture, Melbourne, Australia, 2007.

[2] See section 11 of the *Constitution of the Independent State of Papua New Guinea.*

[3] See section 11(1) of the *Constitution of the Independent State of Papua New Guinea.*

[4] See for example, section 1 of the *Extradition Act 2005.*

[5] See *Application by Gabriel Dusava* (1998) SC581; *Re Calling of Meeting of the Parliament* [1999] PNGLR 285; *Isidore Kaseng v Rabbie Namaliu (No. 1)* [1995] PNGLR 481 and *SCR No. 4 of 1980; Re: Petition of Michael Thomas Somare* [1981] PNGLR 265, per Miles J.

See also: section 11(1) of the *Constitution of the Independent State of Papua New Guinea.*

> and so as not to exceed the authority to make them properly given, to the intent that where any such law would, but for this section, have been in excess to the authority so given it shall nevertheless be a valid law to the extent to which it is not in excess of that authority'.

Whilst the Supreme and National Courts are the guardians of the *Constitution of the Independent State of Papua New Guinea*, it is the responsibility of the Parliament to enact legislation that embodies appropriate safeguards to comply with the requirements of the Constitution.[6]

When a Court is deciding whether a statutory provision is inconsistent with a particular provision of the *Constitution of the Independent State of Papua New Guinea* there is a common law presumption in favour of constitutional validity.[7]

However, the *Constitution of the Independent State of Papua New Guinea* is a superior law to a statute and any statute must be read subject to it.[8] If the statutory provision is inconsistent with the *Constitution of the Independent State of Papua New Guinea* it is, to the extent of the inconsistency:

- invalid;

  and

- ineffective[9],

unless the Act specifically provides otherwise[10].

---

[6] See *Hunter v Southam Inc* [1984] 2 SCR 145 at 169.

[7] See *Re Internal Security Act; Reference by the Ombudsman Commission* [1994] PNGLR 341, [1994] PGSC 9.

See also: *Federal Commissioner of Taxation v Munro* (1926) 38 CLR 153 at 180, per Isaacs J and *Richardson v Forestry Commission* (1988) 164 CLR 261, per Mason CJ and Brennan J at 293.

[8] See *The State and Sali v Sisia* [1987] PNGLR 102, [1987] PGSC 18.

[9] See *The State and Sali v Sisia* [1987] PNGLR 102, [1987] PGSC 18.

See also: section 11(1) of the *Constitution of the Independent State of Papua New Guinea.*

[10] See for example, section 1 of the *Extradition Act 2005.*

INTRODUCTION

Sections 10 and 11 of the *Constitution of the Independent State of Papua New Guinea* are the basis of the principle that an Act of Parliament that contravenes a provision of the Constitution is invalid and ineffective.[11]

Whether it is described as a science or an art, statutory interpretation[12] is of central importance to the daily work of all Courts.[13]

When interpreting a statutory provision[14] consideration must be given to:

- the *Constitution of the Independent State of Papua New Guinea*;
- the *Constitution of the Autonomous Region of Bougainville* as regards the statute law of the Autonomous Region of Bougainville;
- the provisions of the *Interpretation Act* (Ch. 2)[15];
- any definitions of terms in the specific statute under consideration[16];

---

[11] See *Application by Herman Joseph Leahy* (2006) SC885, [2006] PGSC 21 and *SCR No. 2 of 1982; Re Kunangel* [1991] PNGLR 1.

[12] For the purpose of this chapter the term 'statutory interpretation' and not 'statutory construction' is used, notwithstanding that 'statutory construction' covers not only the interpretation of the words in a statute, but also the ascertainment of the true intent of the statute considered in relation to the branch of the law with which it is dealing, see *Berry v British Transport Commission* [1961] 3 All ER 65, per Devlin LJ at 75.

[13] See Speech by The Honorable Justice Murray Gleeson AC, Chief Justice of the High Court of Australia, 'The Meaning Of Legislation: Context, Purpose And Respect For Fundamental Rights', Victoria Law Foundation Oration, Melbourne, Australia, July 2008.

[14] See section 1(1) of the *Interpretation Act* (Ch. 2).

[15] See section 2 of that Act.

An Interpretation Act sets out the working assumptions according to which legislation is framed by Parliament, and applied by the courts, see *Attorney-General (Queensland) v Australian Industrial Relations Commission* (2002) 213 CLR 485 at 492-493.

See also: *Floor v Davis* [1980] AC 695 at 708G.

[16] However, Lord Reid has stated that such definitions have often created more problems than they solve, see *Brutus v Cozens* [1973] AC 854 at 861, [1972] UKHL 6.

When considering that the *Revised Edition of the Laws Act 1973* did not authorise substantive changes to legislation, where a substantive change has occurred, resort may be had to the original legislation for the purposes of interpretation, see *ET and CT v Director of Child Welfare* (1984) N455(L).

- any definitions of terms as provided for in section 3(1) of the *Interpretation Act* (Ch. 2);

- the provisions of the *Interpretation Act No. 7 of 2005* (Autonomous Region of Bougainville)[17] as regards the statute law of the Autonomous Region of Bougainville;

  and

- any relevant common law rules of statutory interpretation[18].

In the interpretation of a statute there are some paramount considerations that must be borne in mind and these are contained in sections 109(4) and 158(2) of the *Constitution of the Independent State of Papua New Guinea.*[19]

Section 109(4) states:

> 'Each law made by Parliament shall receive such fair, large and liberal construction and interpretation as will best ensure the attainment of the object of the law according to its true intent, meaning and spirit, and there is no presumption against extra territorality'.

Section 158(2) states:

> 'In interpreting the law the courts shall give paramount consideration to the dispensation of justice'.

---

[17] There however appears to be no legislative or constitutional authority for this statute to be enacted.

A provincial law that is inconsistent with a National law may be ruled to be unconstitutional, see *Re Forestry Act 1991 and the East New Britain Forestry Operations Control Act 1992* [1992] PNGLR 514, [1992] PGSC 6.

[18] Such rules may also be referred to as common law rules or maxims or cannons of statutory interpretation or construction.

[19] See *SCR No. 5 of 1987; Central Banking (Foreign Exchange and Gold) Regulations (Ch. 138)* [1987] PNGLR 433 at 438, [1987] PGSC 4.

INTRODUCTION

The Court's duty is to give:

- a legislative provision its proper meaning, after carefully considering its purpose and context;

  and

- paramount consideration to the dispensation of justice[20].[21]

Furthermore, section 65(3) of the *Constitution of the Autonomous Region of Bougainville* states:

> 'Each law made by the House of Representatives shall receive such fair, large and liberal interpretation as will best ensure the attainment of the object of the law according to its true intent, meaning and spirit'.

It is generally accepted that legislation is an expression of policy.[22]

In other words, policy is usually translated into Acts of Parliament.[23]

An Act of Parliament is therefore an expression of the will of Parliament.[24]

---

[20] See section 158(2) of the *Constitution of the Independent State of Papua New Guinea.*

[21] See *Salamo Elema, Insurance Commissioner v Pacific MMI Insurance Ltd* (2011) SC1114, [2011] PGSC 9 and *The State v James Yali* (2005) N2932, [2005] PGNC28.

However, the 'slip rule' has no application to the interpretation of legislation, see *Application under section 155(2(b) of the Constitution and In the Matter of Part VIII of the Organic Law on National and Local Level Government Elections; Wari James Vele v Powes Parkop* (2008) SC945, [2008] PGSC 28.

[22] See *Fly River Provincial Government v Pioneer Health Services Limited* (2003) SC705; *The Lawyers Act 1986; In The Matter Of An Application By Roger Gill Maguire For Admission As A Lawyer* (2003) N2466; *Patterson v National Capital District* (2001) N2145; *Graeme Rundle v Motor Vehicles Insurance (PNG) Trust* [1978] PNGLR 44 at 47 and *Anna Wemay and others v Kepas Tumdual* [1978] PNGLR 173 at 176.

[23] See *Fly River Provincial Government v Pioneer Health Services Limited* (2003) SC705; *The Lawyers Act 1986; In The Matter Of An Application By Roger Gill Maguire For Admission As A Lawyer* (2003) N2466; *Patterson v National Capital District* (2001) N2145; *Graeme Rundle v Motor Vehicles Insurance (PNG) Trust* [1978] PNGLR 44 at 47 and *Anna Wemay and others v Kepas Tumdual* [1978] PNGLR 173 at 176.

[24] See *Fothergill v Monarch Airlines Ltd* [1981] AC 251, per Lord Diplock at 279, [1980] 3 WLR 209.

INTRODUCTION

The legislative intention is expressed in the words of the statutory provision.[25]

The Parliament expresses its intention through the meaning of the statutory text it has adopted, understood in the light of its background, purpose and object[26], and surrounding circumstances.[27]

However, no legislation pursues its purposes at all costs. The Parliament has to decide as to what competing values will or will not be sacrificed in the achievement of a particular objective.[28]

The task of the Courts is to interpret the words used by Parliament[29], particularly when considering that Parliament does not speak in vain[30].

The duty of the Courts to ascertain and give effect to the will of the Parliament is to explore the intent of Parliament as expressed in its legislation.[31]

The Courts must give effect to the legislative intention and purpose expressed in the language used in the statute.[32]

However, a Court's interest in the legislator's intention is not an interest in actual 'subjective' intention, but rather a quest for meaning.[33]

---

[25] See *Commissioner General of Internal Revenue and Chief Collector of Taxes v Bougainville Copper Limited* (2008) SC920, [2008] PGSC 13; *Patterson v Lawyers Statutory Committee* (2005) SC822 and *David Toll v Kibi Kara and others* [1990] PNGLR 201.

[26] See section 109(4) of the *Constitution of the Independent State of Papua New Guinea*.

[27] See *Singh v The Commonwealth* (2004) 222 CLR 322, [2004] HCA 43, per Gleeson CJ.

[28] See *Rodriguez v United States* (1987) 480 US 522 at 525-526.

[29] See *Direct United States Cable Co v Anglo American Telegraph Co* (1877) 2 App Cas 394 and *Westminster Bank Limited v Zang* [1966] AC 182, per Lord Reid at 222.

[30] See *Attorney-General of Quebec v Carrières Ste-Thérèse Ltée* [1985] 1 SCR 831 at 838.

[31] See Coke 4 Inst. 330.

See also: *Corocraft Ltd v Pan American Airways Inc* [1968] 3 WLR 714, per Donaldson J at 732; *Stock v Frank Jones (Tiplon) Ltd* [2000] 2 AC 115, per Viscount Dilhorne at 131 and Blackstone, 'Commentaries on the Laws of England', (1765), Volume 1 at 59.

[32] See *Salamo Elema, Insurance Commissioner v Pacific MMI Insurance Ltd* (2011) SC1114, [2011] PGSC 9 and *Gari Baki v Allan Kopi* (2008) N4023.

[33] See Speech by The Honorable Justice Susan Crennan AC, Justice of the High Court of Australia, 'Blackstone's "signs" and statutory interpretation', Victoria Bar Continuing Legal Education Lecture, Melbourne, Australia, 2007.

INTRODUCTION

'Intention of the Legislature' is a common, but very slippery phrase.[34]

The concept of legislative intention describes an attributed intention based on inferences drawn from the statute itself.[35]

What is involved is the search for an 'objective' intention of Parliament, not the 'subjective' intention of Ministers or parliamentarians.[36]

Statutory interpretation is a function of the Courts which sometimes leads to accusations that individual judges, under the guise of construing a statute, are in truth legislating from the bench by amending it.[37]

Care must be exercised to ensure that the Courts do not devolve into the sphere of law-making in the disguise of statutory interpretation.[38]

There is no dispute that the duty and power of the Courts is to interpret and apply the law as is laid by Parliament. Then given the well accepted principle of separation of powers between the three arms of government namely:

- the Legislature;
- the Executive;

  and
- the Judiciary,

the Courts should be careful not to enter into the sphere of Parliament when considering the interpretation of the provisions of a statute.[39]

---

[34] See *Salomon v Salomon and Co Ltd* [1897] AC 22, per Lord Watson at 38.

[35] See *Mills v Meeking* (1990) 169 CLR 214 at 226.

[36] See *Eastman v R* (2000) 203 CLR 1, per McHugh J at 146-147 and *HKSAR v Cheung Kwun Yin* [2009] HKCFA 66.

[37] See Speech by The Honorable Justice Murray Gleeson AC, Chief Justice of the High Court of Australia, 'Judicial Legitimacy', Australian Bar Association Conference, New York, USA, July 2000.

[38] See *R H Rayner (Mincing Lane) Ltd v The Chief Collector of Taxes* [1993] PNGLR 416 and *Cooper Brookes (Wollongong) Pty Ltd v Federal Commissioner of Taxation* (1981) 147 CLR 297 at 304.

[39] See *The State v Japhet Marshall Ano* (2007) N3465, [2007] PGNC 162.

INTRODUCTION

Questions relating to statutory interpretation are notorious for generating opposing answers, none of which are clearly right or wrong. Frequently, there is simply no 'right' or 'wrong' answer.[40]

A statute must be construed on the prima facie basis that its provisions are intended to give effect to harmonious goals.[41]

The Parliament must be presumed to have intended a 'certain and predictable' statutory scheme.[42]

Whilst it may be assumed that Parliament does not make mistakes when enacting legislation[43], Parliament does occasionally make mistakes[44].

However, it is not the function of any Court to amend legislation.[45]

---

[40] See *News Ltd v South Sydney District Rugby League Football Club Ltd* (2003) 77 ALJR 1515 at 1524, (2003) 200 ALR 157 at 168.

[41] See *Ross v R* (1979) 141 CLR 432, per Gibbs J at 440.

[42] See *R v Hammersmith and Fulham London Borough Council; ex parte Burkett* [2002] 1 WLR 1593, per Lord Steyne at 1608.

[43] See *SCR No. 4 of 1985; Omaro Garo v The Police* [1985] PNGLR 320, per Kidu CJ at 322, [1985] PGSC 4; *SCR No. 5 of 1987; Central Banking (Foreign Exchange and Gold) Regulations (Ch. 138)* [1987] PNGLR 433, [1987] PGSC 4 and *The State v Francis Angosiwen (No. 2)* (2004) N2670.

See also: *Commissioner for Special Purposes of the Income Tax v Pemsel* [1891] AC 531, per Lord Halsbury LC at 549.

[44] See *The State v Francis Angosiwen (No. 2)* (2004) N2670.

[45] See *Black-Clawson International Ltd v Papierwerke Waldhof-Aschaffenburg Attorney-General* [1975] AC 591 at 613 and 645.

See also: *Stock v Frank Jones (Tipton) Ltd* [1978] 1 WLR 231 at 236, [1978] 1 All ER 948 at 952; *Re Bolton; ex parte Douglas Beane* (1987) 162 CLR 514 at 518, [1987] HCA 12 and *Byrne v Australian Airlines Ltd* (1995) 185 CLR 410 at 459.

INTRODUCTION

Statutory provisions can be interpreted by the use of well-known rules of statutory interpretation.[46]

However, those rules are only flexible guides, and are not part of the substantive law.[47]

It is for the Court who must decide the weight to be given to each of them.[48]

Care must always be taken when applying any rule of statutory interpretation so as not to stray from the language used by Parliament.[49]

When interpreting a statute a Court is not confined to the language of the statute. A Court may look at the substance and effect of the statute.[50]

The words used, even in their literal sense, are the primary and ordinarily the most reliable, source of interpreting the meaning of any writing: be it a statute, a contract or anything else.[51]

---

[46] See *Maunsell v Olins* [1974] 3 WLR 835, per Lord Reid at 837, [1975] AC 373.

See also: *Howard v Commissioners of Public Works* [1994] 1 IR 101, per Blayney J at 151.

An example of such a common law rule of statutory interpretation or maxim is the 'ex expressio unius est exclusio alterius' rule which states that where a provision expressly covers one situation and does not mention another situation, it is to be taken not to catch the other situation.

[47] See *Soso Tumu for Luhalipu Clan and others v Independent State of Papua New Guinea and others* (2002) N2190; *SCR No. 1 of 1985; Inakambi Singorom v Klaut* [1985] PNGLR 238 and *J H Rayner (Mincing Lane) Limited v The Chief Collector of Taxes* [1993] PNGLR 416 at 422.

Each principle of statutory interpretation is a valuable servant, but a dangerous master, see *Houssein v Under Secretary of Industrial Relations and Technology (New South Wales)* (1982) 148 CLR 88 at 94, [1982] HCA 2 and *Colquhoun v Brooks* (1888) 21 QBD 52 at 65.

See also: *Saraswati v R* (1991) 172 CLR 1 at 23-24, [1991] HCA 21.

[48] See *Maunsell v Olins* [1975] AC 373, per Lord Reid at 382, [1974] 3 WLR 835.

[49] See *Black-Clawson International Ltd v Papierwerke Waldhof-Aschaffenburg Attorney-General* [1975] AC 591 at 613.

See also: *Regional Director of Education, Metropolitan East, Department of Education, New South Wales v International Grammar School Sydney Ltd* (1986) 7 NSWLR 302 at 308; *Yuill v Corporate Affairs Commission of New South Wales* (1990) 20 NSWLR 386 and *Gibbs v State of New South Wales* (1990) 21 NSWLR 416.

[50] See *R v Hunt* (1987) Cr App R 180.

[51] As stated by Hand J in *Cabell v Markham* (1945) 148 F 2d (2nd Cir) 737 at 739.

INTRODUCTION

When interpreting the meaning of any word or phrase in a statute the first question to ask always is:

> what is the natural or plain and ordinary meaning of that word or phrase in its context in the statute,

by applying the 'literal rule'.[52]

Where the meaning of the words used in a statute is clear with no ambiguity[53] then the statutory intention must be found within those words.[54]

---

[52] See *Pinner v Everett* [1969] 1 WLR 993, per Lord Reid at 999.

[53] The term 'ambiguity' is often used in a general sense of indicating any situation in which the scope and applicability of a particular statute is, for whatever reason, doubtful, see *Repatriation Commissioner v Vietnam Veterans Association of New South Wales Branch* (2000) 24 NSWLR 548.

The term 'ambiguity' is fairly self-explanatory - it applies to a situation where the meaning of a statutory provision, in relation to the facts of the instant case, is unclear, see Statutory Drafting and Interpretation, Report on: Plain Language and the Law [2000] IELRC 61, paragraph 2.04.

[54] See *The State and others v John Talu Tekwie* (2006) SC843, [2006] PGSC 13; *Application pursuant to section 155(4) by John Mua Nilkare* (1997) SC536; *J H Rayner (Mincing Lane) Limited v The Chief Collector of Taxes* [1993] PNGLR 416 at 422; *Wemas v Kepas Tumdual* [1978] PNGLR 173, per Wilson J at 176; *SCR No. 6 of 1984; Re Provocation* [1985] PNGLR 31, [1985] PGSC 21; *The State v Francis Angosiwen (No. 1)* (2004) N2669; *Rabaul Shipping Limited v Rita Ruru* (2000) N2022; *Thomas Kaidiman v Papua New Guinea Electricity Commission* (2002) N2343 and *Lepanding Singut v Kelly Kinamun and others, Albo Enterprises Pty Ltd, Fedelis Agin, Papua New Guinea Banking Corporation, Paul Piru and John Kil* (2003) N2499.

See also: *Croxford v Universal Insurance Co* [1936] 2 KB 233 at 281; *Mahabir v Chan Wing Motors Limited* [1982] SILR 19 at 21; *Howard v Commissioners of Public Works* [1994] 1 IR 101; *Macarthys Ltd v Smith* [1979] 3 All ER 325 at 332 and *Re Bolton; ex parte Douglas Beane* (1987) 162 CLR 514 at 518, [1987] HCA 12.

INTRODUCTION

If the words of a statute are precise and unambiguous[55], then no more is necessary than to expound those words in their ordinary and natural sense.[56]

There is no need for the Court to engage in any statutory interpretation exercise.[57]

However, if the meaning leads to some result that cannot reasonably be supposed to have been the intention of the Parliament then it is proper to look for some other possible meaning of the word or phrase.[58]

The purpose of words or phrases used in question should be read and construed in the context of the provision as a whole. The Court should avoid a technical or legalistic construction of words and phrases used in a statutory provision without regard to other provisions which give context and meaning to the particular word(s) and phrases in question.[59]

However, if the words are not so clear or ambiguous, the Court must:

- construe the words in a fair and liberal manner in ascertaining their meaning;

  and

---

[55] The word 'ambiguity' is often used in a general sense as indicating any situation in which the scope and applicability of a particular statute is, for whatever reason, doubtful, see *Repatriation Commissioner v Vietnam Veterans Association of New South Wales Branch* (2000) 24 NSWLR 548.

Refer also to: Report on Statutory Drafting and Interpretation: Plain Language and the Law [2000] IELRC 61, paragraph 2.04.

[56] See *The State and others v John Talu Tekwie* (2006) SC843, [2006] PGSC 13; *J H Rayner (Mincing Lane) Limited v The Chief Collector of Taxes* [1993] PNGLR 416 at 422; *Wemas v Kepas Tumdual* [1978] PNGLR 173, per Wilson J at 176 and *SCR No. 6 of 1984; Re Provocation* [1985] PNGLR 31, [1985] PGSC 21.

See also: *Croxford v Universal Insurance Co* [1936] 2 KB 233 at 281; *Mahabir v Chan Wing Motors Limited* [1982] SILR 19 at 21; *Howard v Commissioners of Public Works* [1994] 1 IR 101; *Macarthys Ltd v Smith* [1979] 3 All ER 325 at 332 and *Re Bolton; ex parte Douglas Beane* (1987) 162 CLR 514 at 518, [1987] HCA 12.

[57] See *Salamo Elema, Insurance Commissioner v Pacific MMI Insurance Ltd* (2011) SC1114, [2011] PGSC 9 and *Gari Baki v Allan Kopi* (2008) N4023.

[58] See *Pinner v Everett* [1969] 1 WLR 993, per Lord Reid at 999.

[59] See *Salamo Elema, Insurance Commissioner v Pacific MMI Insurance Ltd* (2011) SC1114, [2011] PGSC 9 and *Gari Baki v Allan Kopi* (2008) N4023.

- give an interpretation which gives meaning and effect to the legislative intention in the provision.[60]

In such cases a Court is entitled to prefer the interpretation that grants justice and avoids anomaly and absurdity since the Parliament never intended injustice or absurdity when it made the law in the first place.[61]

Courts are no longer satisfied with a literal or grammatical meaning of words that do not conform to the presumed legislative intention, including the policy that can be discerned from the law in question.[62]

The literal meaning should also not be used if it leads to a result:

- unintended by the legislature;

  or

- that runs counter to the dispensation of justice.[63]

In such cases the Courts apply the 'purposive rule' of statutory interpretation.

---

[60] See *Salamo Elema, Insurance Commissioner v Pacific MMI Insurance Ltd* (2011) SC1114, [2011] PGSC 9; *Gari Baki v Allan Kopi* (2008) N4023 and *The State v James Yali* (2005) N2932, [2005] PGNC28.

[61] See *SCR No. 6 of 1984; Re Provocation* [1985] PNGLR 31, [1985] PGSC 21; *Anna Wemay and others v Kepas Tumdual* [1978] PNGLR 173 at 176 and *J H Rayner (Mincing Lae) Limited v The Chief Collector of Taxes* [1993] PNGLR 416 at 422.

See also: *Applin v Race Relations Board* [1974] 2 WLR 541; *Director of Public Prosecutions (Nauru) v Michael Fowler* (1984) 154 CLR 627, [1984] HCA 48; *Cooper Brookes (Woollongong) Pty Ltd v Federal Commissioner of Taxation* (1981) 147 CLR 297, per Gibbs ACJ at 304; *Kaporonovski v R* (1973) 133 CLR 209, per Gibbs J at 238; *Stock v Frank Jones (Tipton) Ltd* [1978] 1 WLR 231, [1978] 1 All ER 948, per Lord Scarman at 238 and 955; *Camden London Borough Council v Post Office* [1977] 1 WLR 892, per Lord Denning at 897; *Magin v Commissioner of Inland Revenue* [1971] NZLR 591; *Johnson v Moreton* [1978] 3 WLR 538; *Re Application by the Minister for Western Provincial Affairs* [1983] SILR 141 at 143-148; *Solomon Breweries Limited v Controller of Customs and Excise* [2000] SBHC 97 and *Northman v Barnet London Borough Council* [1978] 1 WLR 220, per Lord Denning at 228.

[62] See *Cooper Brookes (Wollongong) Pty Ltd v Federal Commissioner of Taxation* (1981) 147 CLR 297 at 321.

[63] See *The State v James Yali* (2005) N2932, [2005] PGNC28.

INTRODUCTION

The purposive, and not a literal, approach[64] is the method of statutory construction that now prevails in such cases.[65]

The mere fact that Parliament may have thought that the law was one thing does not preclude a Court deciding that it is another.[66]

However, a statutory provision cannot be disregarded on the suggested ground that it was made as a result of incorrect information.[67]

---

[64] See *PLAR No. 1 of 1980; Request by Principal Legal Advisor on a Point of Law arising in a case where a person tried upon indictment has been acquitted* [1980] PNGLR 326, [1980] PGSC 15.

See also: *Fothergill v Monarch Airlines Ltd* [1981] AC 251 at 272-273, 275, 280 and 290, [1980] 3 WLR 209.

[65] Whilst the 'literal rule' is concerned with the meaning of words and phrases, the 'purposive rule' is concerned with the overall result that the statute seeks to achieve, see 'Report on Statutory Drafting and Interpretation: Plain Language and the Law' [2000] IELRC 61, paragraph 1.03.

Refer also to: The Law Reform Commission of Hong Kong, 1997, 'Report on Extrinsic Materials as an Aid to Statutory Interpretation', paragraph 1.5.

[66] See *Birmingham Corporation v West Midland Baptist Trust Association (Inc)* [1970] AC 874, per Lord Reid at 898.

[67] See *Labrador Co v R* [1893] AC 104 and *Hoani Te Heuheu Teukino v Aotea District Maori Land Board* [1941] AC 308.

GENERAL LAW-MAKING POWERS

[1.0] NATIONAL PARLIAMENT

The *Constitution of the Independent State of Papua New Guinea* provides:

- that the Parliament may make laws for the peace, order and good governance of Papua New Guinea and the welfare of the people[68];

  and

- that subject to that Constitution, the legislative power of the People is vested in the National Parliament[69].

[2.0] HOUSE OF REPRESENTATIVES OF THE AUTONOMOUS REGION OF BOUGAINVILLE

The *Constitution of the Autonomous Region of Bougainville* provides that:

- subject to any change in the status of Bougainville that Constitution is the supreme law of Bougainville[70];

  and

- all Bougainville laws and all acts that are inconsistent with that Constitution are, to the extent of the inconsistency, invalid and ineffective[71].

---

[68] See section 109(1).

However, there is no enforceable duty owed by the Parliament or its members to act constitutionally, see *Rediffusion (Hong Kong) Ltd v Attorney-General (Hong Kong)* [1970] AC 1136.

Whilst the legislature cannot be restrained from passing an unconstitutional statute [see *Hughes Vale Pty Ltd v Gair* (1950) 90 CLR 203 at 205 and *Harris v Adeang* [1998] NRSC 1], such a statute can be ruled to be inconsistent with the *Constitution of the Independent State of Papua New Guinea* by the Supreme Court, and therefore ruled to be invalid and ineffective [see sections 10 and 18(1), but subject to section 109(3)].

[69] See section 100(1).

[70] See sections 206(2) and 286(1).

[71] See sections 206(2) and 213.

GENERAL LAW-MAKING POWERS

Subject to section 291(4) of the *Constitution of the Independent State of Papua New Guinea*, the Bougainville Government has the power to:

- adopt the *Criminal Code* (Ch. 262);

- create and set penalties or offences incidental to the exercise of its agreed powers and functions;

- amend National laws relating to summary offences and other laws relating to criminal law as they apply in Bougainville;

  and

- make laws relating to criminal law, other than a law equivalent to the *Criminal Code* (Ch. 262).[72]

National laws relating to the functions and power available to the Bougainville Government shall continue to apply until replaced by Bougainville laws[73].

The *Constitution of the Autonomous Region of Bougainville* provides that:

- subject to this Constitution and the Bougainville laws, the House of Representatives of the Autonomous Region of Bougainville may make laws for the peace, order and good government of the Autonomous Region of Bougainville[74];

- subject to section 155, any member of the House of Representatives is entitled to introduce a Bill into the House of Representatives[75];

  and

- the legislative power of the Autonomous Bougainville Government is vested in the House of Representatives[76].

---

[72] See section 291(2) of the *Constitution of the Independent State of Papua New Guinea*, but subject to subsection (4).

[73] See section 296(1) of the *Constitution of the Independent State of Papua New Guinea*.

[74] See section 65(1).

[75] See section 67.

[76] See section 54(1).

LEGISLATIVE PROCEDURE

[1.0] NATIONAL PARLIAMENT

When an Act is initially written it is called a Bill which contains 'clauses' and not 'sections'. The appearance of a Bill is however similar to that of an Act.

Usually a Bill is drafted by the Office of the Legislative Council from a proposal from the National Executive Council[77].

A Bill for an Act is proposed legislation.[78]

During the course of writing a Bill a number of drafts may have been written prior to it receiving the requisite approval from the National Executive Council.

After receiving the approval from the National Executive Council the Bills and Papers Division arranges for the printing of the Bill with explanatory notes and distributes such material to the Members of Parliament.

Explanatory notes are issued by the government department responsible for the administration of the proposed Act. Such notes explain what the Minister and his or her department believes is the purpose of the proposed Act.

The Minister responsible for the Bill will formally present it with the explanatory notes to Parliament, which is referred to as the 'First Reading'.

The Opposition and interested parties are then generally given an opportunity to consider the Bill. It is then arranged for a suitable time to commence parliamentary debate in respect of the Bill. During the course of such debate the intention of the proposed Act should become clear.

The Minister responsible in the course of his or her Second Reading Speech will be expected to explain the provisions of the Bill in some limited detail. Amendments may be voted on and passed or rejected at this stage. That process is formally referred to as the 'Second Reading'.

During the course of the parliamentary debate a Bill can be referred to a parliamentary committee[79], or to Parliament as a Committee of the Whole, for further discussion. A report from the parliamentary committee is then made to Parliament.

---

[77] See section 149 of the *Constitution of the Independent State of Papua New Guinea*.

[78] See *Four Questions Referred under Article 55 of the Constitution* [1969-1982] NLR (Part A) 83, [1977] NRSC 6.

[79] See sections 118 and 121 of the *Constitution of the Independent State of Papua New Guinea*.

During the course of the 'Third Reading' at some later time:

- debate may continue;

  and

- the Bill is voted on[80] and either passed or rejected.

A failure to comply with the relevant provisions of the *Interpretation Act* (Ch. 2) can result in a Court ruling that an Act is invalid.[81]

Making or passing an Act is one thing. Getting it to commence operation is another. It is up to the Parliament to determine the mechanism by which an Act commences operation. The Parliament can fix a specific date, which might be before or after the date on which an Act is passed. The Parliament might delegate the decision about when the Act is to commence operation to a Minister. The Parliament can decide that some parts of an Act will commence operation on one date and other parts will start on another date. Often the Act will state that it will come into operation in accordance with a notice published in the *National Gazette*. If the Act does not say anything on this subject, it comes into operation on the date that is certified by the Speaker in accordance with section 110(1) of the *Constitution of the Independent State of Papua New Guinea*.[82]

[2.0] HOUSE OF REPRESENTATIVES OF THE AUTONOMOUS REGION OF BOUGAINVILLE

Each Bill is drafted by the Office of the Principal Legal Officer from a proposal from:

- the Bougainville Executive Council[83];

  or

---

[80] See section 114 of the *Constitution of the Independent State of Papua New Guinea*.

[81] See *Gath Yasi v Mesi Butu* [1991] PNGLR 206.

[82] See *Mickey Wassey v The Police* (2005) N2922.

See also: Division 5 of Part II of the *Interpretation Act* (Ch. 2).

[83] See section 85 of the *Constitution of the Autonomous Region of Bougainville*.

- an individual member of the House of Representatives[84].

After receiving the approval from the Bougainville Executive Council the Office of the Principal Legal Officer arranges for the printing of the Bill with explanatory notes and distributes such material to the members of the House of Representatives.

Explanatory notes are issued for the administration of the proposed Act. Such notes explain what the Minister and his or her department believes is the purpose of the proposed Act.

The Minister responsible for the Bill will formally present it with the explanatory notes to the House of Representatives, which is referred to as the 'First Reading'.

All members of the House of Representatives are then generally given an opportunity to consider the Bill. It is then arranged for a suitable time to commence parliamentary debate in respect of the Bill. During the course of such debate the intention of the proposed Act should become clear.

The Minister responsible in the course of his or her Second Reading Speech will be expected to explain the provisions of the Bill in some limited detail. Amendments may be voted on and passed or rejected at this stage. That process is formally referred to as the 'Second Reading'.

During the course of the parliamentary debate a Bill can be referred to a parliamentary committee[85] for further discussion. A report from the parliamentary committee is then made to House of Representatives.

During the course of the 'Third Reading' at some later time:

- debate may continue;

  and

- the Bill is voted on and either passed or rejected.

The Speaker shall certify under the Bougainville Seal any law that has been made by the House of Representatives and shall give notification of such laws in the Bougainville Gazette.[86]

A law made by the House of Representatives comes into operation in accordance with the provisions of section 66 of the *Constitution of the Autonomous Region of Bougainville.*

---

[84] See section 67 of the *Constitution of the Autonomous Region of Bougainville.*

[85] See section 71 of the *Constitution of the Autonomous Region of Bougainville.*

[86] See section 66 of the *Constitution of the Autonomous Region of Bougainville.*

PURPOSIVE RULE

When a Court is faced with the task of interpreting and applying the provisions of any legislation, regard must always be had to the intent, meaning and spirit of the legislation in question[87].

This necessarily requires an inquiry as to:

- what was the object or purpose of the legislation?;

  and

- what was the harm or mischief that the Parliament has tried to safeguard against?[88]

It is the duty of a Court in interpreting a statute to suppress the 'mischief'[89] and advance the remedy.[90]

A Court interpreting a statutory provision should strive to give meaning to every word of the provision.[91]

Courts are no longer satisfied with a literal or grammatical meaning of words that do not conform to the presumed legislative intention, including the policy that can be discerned from the law in question.[92]

---

87 See section 109(4) of the *Constitution of the Independent State of Papua New Guinea* and section 65(3) of the *Constitution of the Autonomous Region of Bougainville.*

88 See *Canisius Karingu v Papua New Guinea Law Society* (2010) SC674; *The State v Independent Tribunal; ex parte Sasakila* [1976] PNGLR 491, per Kearney J at 507; *Constitutional Reference No. 1 of 1977* [1977] PNGLR 362, per Prentice DepCJ at 374 and *Moran Development Corporation Ltd v Akida Investments Ltd* (2003) N2458.

89 In *Director of Public Prosecutions (Ivers) v Murphy* [1999] 1 ILRM 46 Denham J commented that the 'mischief rule', in particular, has been subsumed into the 'purposive rule' of statutory interpretation.

90 See *SCR No. 1 of 1981; Re Inter-Group Fighting Act* [1981] PNGLR 151 at 155.

See also: *Magistrates of Glasgow v Police Commissioners of Hillhead* (1885) I 2 R 864 and *Associated Newspapers Group Ltd v Fleming (Inspector of Taxes)* [1973] AC 628, per Lord Simon of Glaisdale at 646.

91 See *R v Berchet* (1688) 1 Show KB 106, 89 ER 480.

See also: *The Commonwealth v Baume* (1905) 2 CLR 405, per Griffith CJ at 414 and O'Connor J at 419 and *Chu Kheng Lim v Minister for Immigration Local Government and Ethnic Affairs* (1992) 176 CLR 1, per Mason CJ at 12-13.

92 See *Cooper Brookes (Wollongong) Pty Ltd v Federal Commissioner of Taxation* (1981) 147 CLR 297 at 321.

PURPOSIVE RULE

The literal meaning should also not be used if it leads to a result:

- unintended by the legislature;

  or

- that runs counter to the dispensation of justice.[93]

In such cases the Courts apply the 'purposive rule' of statutory interpretation.

The purposive, and not a literal, approach[94] is the method of statutory construction that now prevails in such cases.[95]

In such cases statutory interpretation should be:

- purposive;

- contextual[96];

  and

---

[93] See *The State v James Yali* (2005) N2932, [2005] PGNC28.

[94] See *PLAR No. 1 of 1980; Request by Principal Legal Advisor on a Point of Law arising in a case where a person tried upon indictment has been acquitted* [1980] PNGLR 326, [1980] PGSC 15.

See also: *Fothergill v Monarch Airlines Ltd* [1981] AC 251 at 272-273, 275, 280 and 290, [1980] 3 WLR 209.

[95] Whilst the 'literal rule' is concerned with the meaning of words and phrases, the 'purposive rule' is concerned with the overall result that the statute seeks to achieve, see 'Report on Statutory Drafting and Interpretation: Plain Language and the Law' [2000] IELRC 61, paragraph 1.03.

Refer also to: The Law Reform Commission of Hong Kong, 1997, 'Report on Extrinsic Materials as an Aid to Statutory Interpretation', paragraph 1.5.

[96] Refer also to the chapter titled 'Read In Context'.

- holistic[97].[98]

When interpreting a statutory provision 'context' must be considered in the first instance.[99]

A statute should be interpreted in such a way that the object[100] or purpose of the statute is attained. This is what is called the 'purposive rule' of statutory interpretation.

The Courts have favoured this rule of statutory interpretation in their endeavour to achieve substantial justice.[101]

In interpreting the law the Courts must give paramount consideration to the dispensation of justice.[102]

---

97 The meaning of a statutory provision must be determined by reference to the language of the statute viewed as a whole, see *Cooper Brookes (Wollongong) Pty Ltd v Federal Commissioner of Taxation* (1981) 147 CLR 297, per Mason and Wilson JJ at 320; *South West Water Authority v Rumbles* [1985] AC 609, per Lord Scarman at 617 and *Project Blue Sky Inc v Australian Broadcasting Authority* (1998) 194 CLR 355, per McHugh, Gummow, Kirby and Hayne JJ at 381, [1998] HCA 28.

Refer also to the chapter titled 'Read In Context'.

98 See *Medical Council v Chow Siu Shek* (2000) 3 HKCFAR 144 at 154; *Town Planning Board v Society for the Protection of the Harbour Ltd* (2004) 7 HKCFAR 1 at 14; *HKSAR v Lam Kwong Wai* (2006) 9 HKCFAR 574 at 606 and *HKSAR v Cheung Kwun Yin* [2009] HKCFA 66.

99 See *K and S Lake City Freighters Pty Ltd v Gordon and Gotch Ltd* (1985) 157 CLR 309; *CIC Insurance Ltd v Bankstown Football Club Ltd* (1997) 187 CLR 384, [1997] HCA 2; *Project Blue Sky Inc v Australian Broadcasting Authority* (1998) 194 CLR 355, [1998] HCA 28; *Network Ten Pty Ltd v TCN Channel Nine Ltd* (2004) 218 CLR 273, [2004] HCA 14; *Chief Executive Officer of Customs v Granite Arms Pty Ltd* (2005) 222 CLR 149, [2005] HCA 51; *HKSAR v Lam Kwong Wai* (2006) 9 HKCFAR 574, per Sir Mason NPJ at 606 and *Minister for Employment and Workplace Relations v Gribbles Radiology Pty Ltd* (2005) 222 CLR 194.

100 See section 109(4) of the *Constitution of the Independent State of Papua New Guinea*.

101 See *PLAR No. 1 of 1980; Request by Principal Legal Advisor on a Point of Law arising in a case where a person tried upon indictment has been acquitted* [1980] PNGLR 326, [1980] PGSC 15 and *SCR No. 6 of 1984; Re Provocation* [1985] PNGLR 31 at 38-39, [1985] PGSC 21.

See also: *Bermingham v Corrective Services Commission of New South Wales* (1988) 15 NSWLR 292, per McHugh JA at 302 and *Newcastle City Council v GIO General Ltd* (1997) 191 CLR 85, per McHugh J at 113-116, (1997) 149 ALR 623, (1997) 72 ALJR 97, [1997] HCA 53.

102 See section 158(2) of the *Constitution of the Independent State of Papua New Guinea*.

PURPOSIVE RULE

All statutes must be given their fair, large and liberal interpretation so as to best ensure the attainment of the purpose or object of the law according to its Intent, meaning and spirit.[103]

A legislative provision is to be interpreted in such a way to give it effect and meaning consistent with its legislative intent, meaning and spirit.[104]

The statutory provision must be interpreted so that it is consistent with the language and purpose of all the provisions of the statute.[105]

Every word of a statute is presumed to have a role in achieving the objective of the statute. No word or provision should be interpreted so as to render it mere surplusage.[106]

In the interpretation of a provision of a statute, an interpretation that would promote the purpose or object underlying the statute is to be preferred to an interpretation that would not promote that purpose or object.[107]

---

[103] See section 109(4) of the *Constitution of the Independent State of Papua New Guinea* and section 65(3) of the *Constitution of the Autonomous Region of Bougainville.*

See also: *Inakambi Singorom v John Kalaut* [1985] PNGLR 238, per Kidu CJ at 241; *PLAR No. 1 of 1980; Request by Principal Legal Advisor on a Point of Law arising in a case where a person tried upon indictment has been acquitted* [1980] PNGLR 326, [1980] PGSC 15; *Norah Mairi v Alkan Tololo and others* [1976] PNGLR 125 at 136 and *SCR No. 1 of 1978; Ombudsman Commission Investigations of Public Prosecutor* [1978] PNGLR 345, per Pritchard J at 389.

[104] See *Fly River Provincial Government v Pioneer Health Services Limited* (2003) SC705; *Inakambi Singorom v John Kalaut* [1985] PNGLR 238, per Kidu CJ at 241; *PLAR No. 1 of 1980; Request by Principal Legal Advisor on a Point of Law arising in a case where a person tried upon indictment has been acquitted* [1980] PNGLR 326, [1980] PGSC 15; *Norah Mairi v Alkan Tololo and others* [1976] PNGLR 125 at 136; *SCR No. 1 of 1978; Re Ombudsman Commission Investigations of the Public Prosecutor* [1978] PNGLR 345, per Pritchard J at 389 and *Investment Promotion Authority v Niugini Scrap Corporation Pty Ltd; Investment Promotion Authority v James Sinton Spence* (2001) N2104.

[105] See *Inco Europe v First Choice Distribution* [2000] 1 WLR 586, per Lord Nicholls at 592; *Taylor v Public Service Board (New South Wales)* (1976) 137 CLR 208, per Barwick CJ at 213 and *Project Blue Sky Inc v Australian Broadcasting Authority* (1998) 194 CLR 355 at 381-382, [1998] HCA 28.

[106] See *R v Proulx* 2000 SCC 5, [2000] 1 SCR 61; *Rizzo and Rizzo Shoes Ltd (Re)* [1998] 1 SCR 27 and *R v McIntosh* [1995] 1 SCR 686.

[107] See *Nicholls v R* (2005) 219 CLR 196 at 207; *Kelly v R* (2004) 218 CLR 216 at 225-232, [2004] HCA 12 and *Town Planning Board v Society for the Protection of the Harbour Ltd* [2004] HKCFA 27.

PURPOSIVE RULE

In order to interpret a statute in accordance with the purposive rule of statutory interpretation it is sometimes necessary to read the statute as if the statute:

- contained additional words[108];
- had some words omitted[109];

  or

- contained different words[110].[111]

This, however, does not involve the introduction of the words into the statute.[112]

The effect is that as a consequence the statute is read as though it had been amended by the Parliament.

However, a Court should not read into a statute words that are not there, unless this is necessary to give effect to an evident parliamentary intention.[113]

---

108 See *R v Young* (1999) 46 NSWLR 681.

109 See *Inco Europe v First Choice Distribution* [2000] 1 WLR 586, per Lord Nicholls at 592.

110 See *Inco Europe v First Choice Distribution* [2000] 1 WLR 586, per Lord Nicholls at 592.

111 The process of reading down general words is a well-established means of interpretation, see *Bowtell v Goldsborough Mort and Co Ltd* (1906) 3 CLR 444 at 456-457; *Ex parte Walsh and Johnson; Re Yates* (1925) 37 CLR 36 at 91-93; *R v Wilson; ex parte Kisch* (1934) 53 CLR 234 at 244; *Church of the Holy Trinity v United States* (1982) 143 US 457at 459; *Tokyo Mart Pty Ltd v Campbell* (1988) 15 NSWLR 275 at 279; *Smith v East Elloe Rural District Council* [1956] AC 736 at 764-765 and *Bropho v The State of Western Australia* (1991) 171 CLR 1 at 17-18.

112 See *R v Young* (1999) 46 NSWLR 681; *Wentworth Securities Ltd v Jones* [1980] AC 74; *Cooper Brookes (Wollongong) Pty Ltd v Federal Commissioner of Taxation* (1981) 147 CLR 297; *Re Bolton; ex parte Beane* (1987) 162 CLR 514; *Tokyo Mart Pty Ltd v Campbell* (1988) 15 NSWLR 275; *Bermingham v Corrective Services Commission of New South Wales* (1988) 15 NSWLR 292 and *Newcastle City Council v GIO General Ltd* (1997) 191 CLR 85, (1997) 149 ALR 623, (1997) 72 ALJR 97, [1997] HCA 53.

113 See *Thompson v Goold and Co* [1910] AC 409, per Lord Mersey at 420 and *Vickers, Sons and Maxim Ltd v Evans* [1910] AC 444, per Lord Loreburn LC at 445.

See also: *Wills v Bowley* [1983] 1 AC 57 at 78; *Marshall v Watson* (1972) 124 CLR 640 at 649 and *HKSAR v Cheung Kwun Yin* [2009] HKCFA 66.

PURPOSIVE RULE

Prior to a Court applying the purposive rule of statutory interpretation in order to achieve the purpose of the legislative provision by adding words to, omitting words from or substituting words in a statute, the following criteria should be able to be satisfied:

- what was the intended purpose of the statute or provision in question[114], ie., the mischief with which the Act was dealing[115];
- was the mistake made by inadvertence by the legislative draftsperson[116];
- did Parliament fail to give effect to its purpose in the provision in question[117];

---

[114] See *Inco Europe v First Choice Distribution* [2000] 1 WLR 586, per Lord Nicholls at 592; *R (on the application of Kelly and another) v Secretary of State for Justice, Re Gibson* [2008] 3 All ER 844; *R (on the application of Stellato) v Secretary of State for the Home Department* [2007] 2 AC 70; *Lord Chancellor v Haggan* [2007] EWHC 1212 and *Chan Pun Chung and another v HKSAR* [2000] 3 HKLRD 498, per Bokhary PJ at 502-503.

[115] See *Kingston v Keprose Pty Ltd (No. 3)* (1987) 11 NSWLR 404, per McHugh JA at 422; *Jones v Wrotham Park Settled Estates* [1980] AC 74, per Lord Diplock; *Wentworth Securities Ltd v Jones* [1980] AC 74, per Lord Diplock at 105-107; *Bropho v The State of Western Australia* (1991) 171 CLR 1 at 20; *Tokyo Mart Pty Ltd v Campbell* (1988) 15 NSWLR 275, per Mahoney JA at 283; *Bermingham v Corrective Services Commission of New South Wales* (1988) 15 NSWLR 292, per Hope JA at 299-300 and McHugh JA at 302 and *Newcastle City Council v GIO General Ltd* (1997) 191 CLR 85, per McHugh J at 113, (1997) 149 ALR 623, (1997) 72 ALJR 97, [1997] HCA 53.

[116] See *Inco Europe v First Choice Distribution* [2000] 1 WLR 586, per Lord Nicholls at 592; *Kingston v Keprose Pty Ltd (No. 3)* (1987) 11 NSWLR 404, per McHugh JA at 422; *Jones v Wrotham Park Settled Estates* [1980] AC 74, per Lord Diplock; *Wentworth Securities Ltd v Jones* [1980] AC 74, per Lord Diplock at 105-107; *Bropho v The State of Western Australia* (1991) 171 CLR 1 at 20; *Tokyo Mart Pty Ltd v Campbell* (1988) 15 NSWLR 275, per Mahoney JA at 283; *Bermingham v Corrective Services Commission of New South Wales* (1988) 15 NSWLR 292, per Hope JA at 299-300 and McHugh JA at 302; *Newcastle City Council v GIO General Ltd* (1997) 191 CLR 85, per McHugh J at 113, (1997) 149 ALR 623, (1997) 72 ALJR 97, [1997] HCA 53; *R (on the application of Stellato) v Secretary of State for the Home Department* [2007] 2 AC 70; *R (on the application of Kelly and another) v Secretary of State for Justice, Re Gibson* [2008] 3 All ER 844; *Lord Chancellor v Haggan* [2007] EWHC 1212 and *Chan Pun Chung and another v HKSAR* [2000] 3 HKLRD 498 at 502-503.

[117] See *Inco Europe v First Choice Distribution* [2000] 1 WLR 586, per Lord Nicholls at 592; *Kingston v Keprose Pty Ltd (No. 3)* (1987) 11 NSWLR 404, per McHugh JA at 422; *Jones v Wrotham Park Settled Estates* [1980] AC 74, per Lord Diplock; *Wentworth Securities Ltd v Jones* [1980] AC 74, per Lord Diplock at 105-107; *Bropho v The State of Western Australia* (1991) 171 CLR 1 at 20; *Tokyo Mart Pty Ltd v Campbell* (1988) 15 NSWLR 275, per Mahoney JA at 283; *Bermingham v Corrective Services Commission of New South Wales* (1988) 15 NSWLR 292, per Hope JA at 299-300 and McHugh JA at 302; *Newcastle City Council v GIO General Ltd* (1997) 191 CLR 85, per McHugh J at 113, (1997) 149 ALR 623, (1997) 72 ALJR 97, [1997] HCA 53; *R (on the application of Stellato) v Secretary of State for the Home Department* [2007] 2 AC 70; *R (on the application of Kelly and another) v Secretary of State for Justice, Re Gibson* [2008] 3 All ER 844; *Lord Chancellor v Haggan* [2007] EWHC 1212 and *Chan Pun Chung and another v HKSAR* [2000] 3 HKLRD 498 at 502-503.

and

- would the substance of the mistake been amended with certainty had the mistake been noticed.[118]

However, even if those conditions are able to be satisfied a Court may not be able to 'amend' the statute if such an amendment is too far-reaching.[119]

A Court is free to depart from the literal meaning of the words used in a legislative provision, if giving effect to the literal meaning would:

- result in an absurdity;

- lead to a result unintended by the Parliament;

  or

- run counter to the dispensation of justice.[120]

In such circumstances it is the duty of the Court to interpret those words in a fair, large and liberal manner so as to achieve the purpose intended by the Parliament.[121]

---

[118] See *Inco Europe v First Choice Distribution* [2000] 1 WLR 586, per Lord Nicholls at 592; *Kingston v Keprose Pty Ltd (No. 3)* (1987) 11 NSWLR 404, per McHugh JA at 422; *Jones v Wrotham Park Settled Estates* [1980] AC 74, per Lord Diplock; *Wentworth Securities Ltd v Jones* [1980] AC 74, per Lord Diplock at 105-107; *Bropho v The State of Western Australia* (1991) 171 CLR 1 at 20; *Tokyo Mart Pty Ltd v Campbell* (1988) 15 NSWLR 275, per Mahoney JA at 283; *Bermingham v Corrective Services Commission of New South Wales* (1988) 15 NSWLR 292, per Hope JA at 299-300 and McHugh JA at 302; *Newcastle City Council v GIO General Ltd* (1997) 191 CLR 85, per McHugh J at 113, (1997) 149 ALR 623, (1997) 72 ALJR 97, [1997] HCA 53; *R (on the application of Stellato) v Secretary of State for the Home Department* [2007] 2 AC 70; *R (on the application of Kelly and another) v Secretary of State for Justice, Re Gibson* [2008] 3 All ER 844; *Lord Chancellor v Haggan* [2007] EWHC 1212 and *Chan Pun Chung and another v HKSAR* [2000] 3 HKLRD 498, per Bokhary PJ at 502-503.

[119] See *Inco Europe v First Choice Distribution* [2000] 1 WLR 586, per Lord Nicholls at 592.

[120] See *The State v James Yali* (2005) N2932, [2005] PGNC 28.

See also: *Pinner v Everett* [1969] 1 WLR 993, per Lord Reid at 999.

[121] See *Inakambi Singorom v John Kalaut* [1985] PNGLR 238, per Kidu CJ at 241; *PLAR No. 1 of 1980; Request by Principal Legal Advisor on a Point of Law arising in a case where a person tried upon indictment has been acquitted* [1980] PNGLR 326, [1980] PGSC 15; *Norah Mairi v Alkan Tololo and others* [1976] PNGLR 125 at 136 and *SCR No. 1 of 1978; Ombudsman Commission Investigations of Public Prosecutor* [1978] PNGLR 345, per Pritchard J at 389.

PURPOSIVE RULE

Nevertheless a Court should not attribute to a statutory provision a meaning that the language, understood in the light of its context and the statutory purpose, is incapable of meaning.[122]

The application of the purposive rule of statutory interpretation may also be of limited assistance when there is a doubt as to the extent to which some legislation pursues its purpose and when considering that legislation rarely pursues a single purpose at all costs.[123]

Furthermore, the purposive rule of statutory interpretation must not be used by Courts to nullify laws:

- that are clearly constitutional;

  and

- which clearly and unambiguously state the intentions of the Parliament.[124]

[122] See *R v A (No. 2)* [2002] 1 AC 45, per Lord Steyne at 68; *McAlister* (1990) 169 CLR 324 at 330 and *R v Di Maria* (1996) 67 SASR 466 at 472-474.

[123] See *Carr v The State of Western Australia* [2007] HCA 47, per Gleeson CJ.

[124] See *SCR No. 1 of 1985; Inakambi Singorom v Klaut* [1985] PNGLR 238, per Kidu CJ at 241.

READ IN CONTEXT

[1.0] STATUTORY PROVISION

Section 2 of the *Interpretation Act* (Ch. 2) states (in part):

> '(1) Except where in this Act the context indicates otherwise, or some other meaning is clearly intended, this Act applies to every statutory provision (including this Act) whenever made or adopted.
>
> (2) The rules contained in this Act apply in accordance with Subsection (1) unless the context of any particular statutory provision indicates otherwise, or some other meaning is clearly indicated by a particular statutory provision'.

[2.0] GENERAL PRINCIPLES

In law 'context' is everything.[125]

All the words and provisions of a statute must be read in their context.[126]

All words of a statutory provision should be read in their:

- entire[127];

  or

- widest[128]

'context'.

---

[125] See *Liyanage v R* [1967] 1 AC 259.

See also: *R (Daly) v Secretary of State for the Home Department* [2001] 2 AC 532, per Lord Steyne at 548.

[126] See *Elema v MMI Insurance Ltd* (2011) SC1114 and *The State v Alan Bekau* [1982] PNGLR 119, per McDermott AJ at 120-121.

See also: *Hills v Attorney-General of Canada* (1988) 48 DLR (4th) 193, per Lamer J at 196.

[127] See *Rizzo and Rizzo Shoes Ltd (Re)* [1998] 1 SCR 27 and *R v McIntosh* [1995] 1 SCR 686.

[128] See *Attorney-General v Prince Ernest Augustus of Hanover* [1957] AC 436 at 461.

READ IN CONTEXT

When interpreting a statutory provision 'context' must be considered in the first instance.[129]

A Court is permitted, in construing a statutory provision, to have regard to the words used by the Parliament in their legal and historical context and, if appropriate, to give them a meaning that will give effect to any purpose of the legislation that can be deduced from that context.[130]

Definitions of words are to be read subject to anything 'repugnant in the context, or in the sense'.[131]

The meaning of a text is always influenced, and sometimes controlled, by 'context'.[132]

The 'context' includes:

- the general purpose of the legislation[133];

---

[129] See *Toronto Suburban Railway Co v Toronto Corporation* [1915] AC 590 at 597.

See also: *K and S Lake City Freighters Pty Ltd v Gordon and Gotch Ltd* (1985) 157 CLR 309; *CIC Insurance Ltd v Bankstown Football Club Ltd* (1997) 187 CLR 384, [1997] HCA 2; *Project Blue Sky Inc v Australian Broadcasting Authority* (1998) 194 CLR 355, [1998] HCA 28; *Network Ten Pty Ltd v TCN Channel Nine Ltd* (2004) 218 CLR 273, [2004] HCA 14; *Chief Executive Officer of Customs v Granite Arms Pty Ltd* (2005) 222 CLR 149, [2005] HCA 51; *Medical Council of Hong Kong v Chow Siu Shek* (2000) 3 HKCFAR 144 at 154 and *Minister for Lands (New South Wales) v Jeremias* (1917) 23 CLR 322 at 332.

[130] See *CIC Insurance Ltd v Bankstown Football Club Ltd* (1997) 187 CLR 384 at 408, [1997] HCA 2 and *Newcastle City Council v GIO General Ltd* (1997) 191 CLR 85 at 112-113, (1997) 149 ALR 623, (1997) 72 ALJR 97, [1997] HCA 53.

[131] See *Meux v Jacobs* [1875] LR 7 HL 481, per Lord Selborne at 493.

[132] See *Singh v The Commonwealth* (2004) 222 CLR 322 at 332, [2004] HCA 43.

[133] See *Toronto Suburban Railway Co v Toronto Corporation* [1915] AC 590 at 597.

See also: *K and S Lake City Freighters Pty Ltd v Gordon and Gotch Ltd* (1985) 157 CLR 309; *CIC Insurance Ltd v Bankstown Football Club Ltd* (1997) 187 CLR 384, [1997] HCA 2; *Project Blue Sky Inc v Australian Broadcasting Authority* (1998) 194 CLR 355, [1998] HCA 28; *Network Ten Pty Ltd v TCN Channel Nine Ltd* (2004) 218 CLR 273, [2004] HCA 14; *R v Bull* (1974) 131 CLR 203; *Chief Executive Officer of Customs v Granite Arms Pty Ltd* (2005) 222 CLR 149, [2005] HCA 51; *Medical Council of Hong Kong v Chow Siu Shek* (2000) 3 HKCFAR 144 at 154; *Minister for Lands (New South Wales) v Jeremias* (1917) 23 CLR 322 at 332; *Alcan (Northern Territory) Alumina Pty Ltd v Commissioner of Territory Revenue* (2009) 239 CLR 27, [2009] HCA 41 and *Travelex Ltd v Federal Commissioner of Taxation* (2010) 84 ALJR 683, [2010] HCA 33.

- its preamble[134];
- the other enacting provisions of the same statute[135];
- the existing state of the law at the time of enactment, including the common law[136];
- any statutes read 'in pari materia'[137];

---

134 As stated by Lord Simonds in *Attorney-General v Prince Ernest Augustus of Hanover* [1957] AC 436 at 461.

Refer also to the section titled 'Intrinsic Aids' in the chapter titled 'Aids To Interpretation'.

135 As stated by Lord Simonds in *Attorney-General v Prince Ernest Augustus of Hanover* [1957] AC 436 at 461.

136 See *Toronto Suburban Railway Co v Toronto Corporation* [1915] AC 590 at 597 and *Attorney-General v Prince Ernest Augustus of Hanover* [1957] AC 436 at 461.

See also: *AB v Western Australia; AH v Western Australia* [2011] HCA 42; *K and S Lake City Freighters Pty Ltd v Gordon and Gotch Ltd* (1985) 157 CLR 309; *CIC Insurance Ltd v Bankstown Football Club Ltd* (1997) 187 CLR 384, [1997] HCA 2; *Project Blue Sky Inc v Australian Broadcasting Authority* (1998) 194 CLR 355, [1998] HCA 28; *Network Ten Pty Ltd v TCN Channel Nine Ltd* (2004) 218 CLR 273, [2004] HCA 14; *R v Bull* (1974) 131 CLR 203; *Chief Executive Officer of Customs v Granite Arms Pty Ltd* (2005) 222 CLR 149, [2005] HCA 51; *Medical Council of Hong Kong v Chow Siu Shek* (2000) 3 HKCFAR 144 at 154; *Minister for Lands (New South Wales) v Jeremias* (1917) 23 CLR 322 at 332; *Wik Peoples v Queensland* (1996) 187 CLR 1, per Gummow J at 171; *HKSAR v Cheung Kwun Yin* [2009] HKCFA 66 and *Newcastle City Council v GIO General Ltd* (1997) 191 CLR 85 at 112-113, (1997) 149 ALR 623, (1997) 72 ALJR 97, [1997] HCA 53.

137 See *Attorney-General v Prince Ernest Augustus of Hanover* [1957] AC 436 at 461.

See also: *K and S Lake City Freighters Pty Ltd v Gordon and Gotch Ltd* (1985) 157 CLR 309 at 315 and *Wik Peoples v Queensland* (1996) 187 CLR 1, per Gummow J at 171.

Refer also to the section titled 'Extrinsic Aids' in the chapter titled 'Aids To Interpretation'.

- the other provisions of the statute[138];
- the background provided by other legislation[139];
- the legislative history[140], ie., its historical context[141];

  and

- the time, place and any other circumstance that could rationally assist understanding of meaning.

The meaning of a word is not derived by referring to it in isolation from the remainder of the statute.[142]

---

138 See *Toronto Suburban Railway Co v Toronto Corporation* [1915] AC 590 at 597 and *Attorney-General v Prince Ernest Augustus of Hanover* [1957] AC 436 at 461.

See also: *K and S Lake City Freighters Pty Ltd v Gordon and Gotch Ltd* (1985) 157 CLR 309; *CIC Insurance Ltd v Bankstown Football Club Ltd* (1997) 187 CLR 384, [1997] HCA 2; *Project Blue Sky Inc v Australian Broadcasting Authority* (1998) 194 CLR 355, [1998] HCA 28; *Network Ten Pty Ltd v TCN Channel Nine Ltd* (2004) 218 CLR 273, [2004] HCA 14; *R v Bull* (1974) 131 CLR 203; *Chief Executive Officer of Customs v Granite Arms Pty Ltd* (2005) 222 CLR 149, [2005] HCA 51; *Medical Council of Hong Kong v Chow Siu Shek* (2000) 3 HKCFAR 144 at 154; *Minister for Lands (New South Wales) v Jeremias* (1917) 23 CLR 322 at 332 and *HKSAR v Cheung Kwun Yin* [2009] HKCFA 66.

139 See *Toronto Suburban Railway Co v Toronto Corporation* [1915] AC 590 at 597.

140 See *K and S Lake City Freighters Pty Ltd v Gordon and Gotch Ltd* (1985) 157 CLR 309 at 315 and *Wik Peoples v Queensland* (1996) 187 CLR 1, per Gummow J at 171.

Refer also to the section titled 'Extrinsic Aids' in the chapter titled 'Aids To Interpretation'.

141 See *CIC Insurance Ltd v Bankstown Football Club Ltd* (1997) 187 CLR 384 at 408, [1997] HCA 2 and *Newcastle City Council v GIO General Ltd* (1997) 191 CLR 85 at 112-113, (1997) 149 ALR 623, (1997) 72 ALJR 97, [1997] HCA 53.

142 See *Palgo Holdings Pty Ltd v Gowans* (2005) 221 CLR 249; *Collector of Customs v Agfa-Gevaert Ltd* (1996) 186 CLR 389 at 396-397, (1996) 141 ALR 59, (1996) 71 ALJR 123, [1996] HCA 36; *R v Brown* [1996] AC 543 at 561 and *East Donegal Cooperative Marts v Attorney-General* [1970] IR 317, per Walsh J at 314.

READ IN CONTEXT

In order to interpret a particular statutory provision in its 'context' a Court may apply the following common law maxims or rules of statutory interpretation:

- the 'noscitur a sociis' rule which provides that a word or phrase should be interpreted whilst taking into consideration the other words or phrases that surround it;

  and

- the 'ejusdem generis' or 'class rule', often known as the rule in Heydon's case[143], which provides that where in a statute there are general words following particular and specific words, the general words must be confined to things of the same kind as those specified.[144]

To read a section in isolation from the statute of which it forms a part is to offend against the cardinal rule of statutory interpretation that requires the words of a statute to be read in their 'context'.[145]

Although generally in construing a statute words should be given their plain and ordinary meaning, the 'context' may indicate that a word is intended to have another meaning.[146]

A certain word used in a statute may have several meanings. However, when that word is considered within the 'context' in which it is found, in the section or within the scheme of the whole Act, then the true or correct meaning should become apparent. A common phrase often heard is that 'words must be read within their context' or the 'Act must be read as a whole'.[147]

---

143 (1584) 3 Co. Rep. 7a.

144 See *Dean v Attorney-General of Queensland* [1971] Qd R 391, per Stable J at 403.

This rule of statutory interpretation is also examined in the chapter titled 'Meaning Of Words And Phrases'.

145 See *K and S Lake City Freighters Pty Ltd v Gordon and Gotch Ltd* (1985) 60 ALR 509, per Mason J at 514.

146 See *Dekarube v Agieroudi* [1975] NRSC 2.

147 See *Mamaloni v Attorney-General and the Governor-General* [1993] SBHC 71.

READ IN CONTEXT

A statute should be interpreted as a whole so far as possible by construing not just one phrase or section, but the whole of the statute.[148]

The importance of ensuring that words and phrases are interpreted according to their 'context' should not be underestimated simply because the context of words or phrases may vary from statute to statute. In some instances a word or phrase may be given a 'deemed' meaning and therefore, such a word or phrase should not be given its plain and ordinary meaning.

The true significance of a word must depend on the 'context' in which the word is used, and not necessarily referring to the meaning of the word in other statutes.[149]

A Court should not attribute to a statutory provision a meaning that the language, understood in the light of its 'context' and the statutory purpose, is incapable of meaning.[150]

---

[148] See *Luke Tai v Australia and New Zealand Banking Group (PNG) Limited* (2000) N1979 and *Minister For Lands v Frame* [1980] PNGLR 433 at 453.

See also: *Cooper Brookes (Wollongong) Pty Ltd v Federal Commissioner of Taxation* (1981) 147 CLR 297, per Mason and Wilson JJ at 320; *South West Water Authority v Rumbles* [1985] AC 609, per Lord Scarman at 617; *Project Blue Sky Inc v Australian Broadcasting Authority* (1998) 194 CLR 355, per McHugh, Gummow, Kirby and Hayne JJ at 381, [1998] HCA 28 and *Williamson Pty Ltd v Barrowcliff* [1915] Vic Law Rp 66; [1915] VLR 450, per Hodges J.

[149] See *Seal (PNG) Pty Ltd and others v Superintendent of Motor Traffic and The Independent State of Papua New Guinea* (1997) N1638.

[150] See *R v A (No. 2)* [2002] 1 AC 45, per Lord Steyne at 68; *McAlister* (1990) 169 CLR 324 at 330 and *R v Di Maria* (1996) 67 SASR 466 at 472-474.

AIDS TO INTERPRETATION

[1.0] INTRODUCTION

Courts may use aids in order to interpret a statutory provision.

Such aids are:

- 'intrinsic aids', also referred to as 'internal aids'[151];

  and

- extrinsic aids.

However, secondary material seeking to explain the meaning of the words of a statute cannot displace the clear meaning of the text of a provision.[152]

The following are not considered as aids, and therefore should not be used in the interpretation of a statutory provision:

- **Bill**[153];

- **Heading to a section**

  Section 26(3) of the *Interpretation Act* (Ch. 2) states:

  > 'The heading [...] to the various sections of a statutory provision do not form part of the provision'.

- **Head-note to a section**

  Section 26(3) of the *Interpretation Act* (Ch. 2) states:

  > 'The [...] head-notes to the various sections of a statutory provision do not form part of the provision'.

---

[151] See The Law Reform Commission of Hong Kong, 1997, 'Report on Extrinsic Materials as an Aid to Statutory Interpretation', page 3.

[152] See *Northern Territory v Collins* (2008) 235 CLR 619 at 623 and 642, [2008] HCA 49.

[153] See *Commissioner for Prices and Consumer Affairs v Charles Moore (Australia) Pty Ltd* (1977) 139 CLR 449, (1977) 14 ALR 485.

See however: *Duggan v Mirror Newspapers Ltd* (1978) 142 CLR 583, (1978) 22 ALR 439.

- **Marginal Note**[154]

  Section 26(4) of the *Interpretation Act* (Ch. 2) states:

  > 'Marginal notes [...] to a statutory provision do not form part of the provision'.

- **Footnote**[155]

  Section 26(4) of the *Interpretation Act* (Ch. 2) states:

  > '[...] footnotes to a statutory provision do not form part of the provision'.

- **Explanatory Memorandum**[156]

  An explanatory memorandum is :

  - a document that summarises the subject matter of a Bill;

    and

  - prepared primarily for the information of members of Parliament.[157]

---

[154] See *Cork County Council v Whillock* [1993] 1 IR 231.

See however: *Dougherty and Co Ltd v Allen Ltd* [1985] IR 340; *Cox v Ireland* [1992] 2 IR 503; *Attorney-General v Thornton* [1964] IR 458 and *Director of Public Prosecutions v Judge O'Buachalla and Mulhall* [1999] 1 ILRM 362.

[155] See *Cork County Council v Whillock* [1993] 1 IR 231.

See however: *Dougherty and Co Ltd v Allen Ltd* [1985] IR 340; *Cox v Ireland* [1992] 2 IR 503; *Attorney-General v Thornton* [1964] IR 458 and *Director of Public Prosecutions v Judge O'Buachalla and Mulhall* [1999] 1 ILRM 362.

[156] See *Escoigne Properties Ltd v I.L.C.* [1958] AC 549.

See also: *Re Jauncey* [1980] Qd R 335 at 336-342; *Administration of Norfolk Island v Walsh* [2005] NFC 6; *Inglis v British Airport Authority* [1978] SLT 30 and *Re Shang Kiang-Yuen, A Patient* [1968] HKLR 192 at 200-201.

See however: *HKSAR v Cheung Kwun Yin* [2009] HKCFA 66; *Maher v Attorney-General* [1973] IR 140; *McLoughlin v Minister for the Public Service* [1985] IR 631; *Ealing London Borough Council v Race Relations Board* [1972] AC 342 at 361; *Elson-Vernon Knitters Ltd v Sino-Indo-American Spinners Ltd* [1972] HKLR 468 and *Fung v First Pacific Bank Ltd* [1989] 2 HKLR 614.

[157] See The Law Reform Commission of Hong Kong, 1997, 'Report on Extrinsic Materials as an Aid to Statutory Interpretation', page 21.

Furthermore, direct evidence from a public servant as to the policy of any particular legislation is also unlikely to be helpful in the process of statutory interpretation.[158]

[2.0] INTRINSIC AIDS

The phrase 'intrinsic aids' refers to:

> any material which is published with an Act, but does not refer to a substantive provision of an Act.[159]

Such aids include:

- **Long Title, Short Title and Preamble**

  The enacting provisions of a statute, long title and the preamble[160] may be used as an aid in interpretation.[161]

  Section 24A of the *Interpretation Act* (Ch. 2) states (in part):

  > 'The short title [and] long title [...] of a provision are those portions of a provision illustrated in Schedule 3 and designated in the schedule or by the footnotes to that schedule'.

  As regards the *Summary Offences Act* (Ch. 264):

  - the 'short title' is '*Summary Offences Act 1977* (Ch. 264);

    and

  - the 'long title' is 'Being an Act relating to summary offences'.

[158] See *Collector of Customs v Savage River Mines* (1988) 79 ALR 258 at 263.

[159] See Report on Statutory Drafting and Interpretation: Plain Language and the Law [2000] IELRC 61, paragraph 4.01.

[160] As stated by Lord Simonds in *Attorney-General v Prince Ernest Augustus of Hanover* [1957] AC 436 at 461.

[161] See *Attorney-General v Prince Ernest Augustus of Hanover* [1957] AC 436.

The short title and long title are the plainest of all guides to the general objectives of a statute.[162]

However, the short title has no interpretative weight; it provides only a mode of citation.[163]

It is proper for a Court to look at the long title for the purpose of determining the scope of a statute; it may be referred to, not to contradict any clear and unambiguous language, but if there is any uncertainty it may be referred to for the purpose of resolving the uncertainty.[164]

- **Heading of a Chapter, Part, Division and Subdivision**

  Section 26(1) of the *Interpretation Act* (Ch. 2) states:

  > 'The headings of the Chapters, Parts, Divisions and Subdivisions into which a statutory provision is divided form part of the provision.
  >
  > Headings have been held to form part of the context in which the enacting sections may be interpreted.[165]
  >
  > However, if the words of a section are clear then their meaning takes precedence over the meaning of the heading, even if it suggests a different meaning.[166]

---

[162] See *The State v Danny Sunu and others* [1983] PNGLR 396 at 402.

See also: *Director of Public Prosecutions v Quilligan* [1987] ILRM 606 at 635 and *Black-Clawson International Ltd v Papierwerke Waldhof-Aschaffenburg Attorney-General* [1975] AC 591 at 647.

[163] See *Re Boaler* [1915] 1 KB 21 at 27.

[164] See *Birch v Allen* (1942) 65 CLR 621, per Latham CJ at 625; *East Donegal Co-operative Marts v Attorney General* [1970] IR 317; *Director of Public Prosecutions v Quilligan* [1987] ILRM 606 at 635 and *Black-Clawson International Ltd v Papierwerke Waldhof-Aschaffenburg Attorney-General* [1975] AC 591 at 647.

[165] See *Pax v Surrey (North Eastern Area) Assessment Committee* [1948] 1 KB 29, per Goddard LCJ at 32 and *Qualter Hall and Co Ltd v Board of Trade* [1961] Ch 121 at 131.

See also: *Magistrates of Buckie v The Dowager Countess of Seafeld's Trustees* [1928] SC 525.

[166] See *Fletcher v Birkenhead Corporation* [1907] 1 KB 205, per Farwell LJ at 218 and *R v Surrey (North Eastern Area) Assessment Committee* [1948] 1 KB 28, per Goddard LCJ at 32-33.

See also: *Lee Vanit v R* (1997) 72 ALJR 1, [1997] HCA 51.

AIDS TO INTERPRETATION

- **Interpretation Section**[167]

  The function of a definition is not to enact substantive law, but to provide an aid in construing a statute.[168]

  Therefore, a Court may:

  - refer to the 'Interpretation' section/s in the statute in question.

    The purpose of a definition in a statute is to limit or modify the ordinary and natural meaning of a word.[169]

    Therefore, when particular words or phrases the subject of a definition section are found in a statute such words and phrases are to be understood in the defined sense.[170]

  - refer to section 3(1) of the *Interpretation Act* (Ch. 2).[171]

    That section provides the definitions of a number of words and phrases and commences with the words:

    > 'In any statutory provision'.

    That section contains definitions of words and phrases that are deemed to apply in any other statutory provision.[172]

---

[167] Refer also to the chapter titled 'Meaning Of Words And Phrases'.

[168] As noted by McHugh J in *Kelly v R* (2004) 218 CLR 216, [2004] HCA 12.

[169] See *Brutus v Cozens* [1973] AC 854, [1972] UKHL 6.

[170] See *Gibb v Commissioner of Taxation* (1966) 118 CLR 628 at 634, [1967] ALR 527.

[171] An Interpretation Act sets out the working assumptions according to which legislation is framed by Parliament, and applied by the courts, see *Attorney-General (Queensland) v Australian Industrial Relations Commission* (2002) 213 CLR 485 at 492-493.

See also: *Floor v Davis* [1980] AC 695 at 708.

[172] See section 2 of the *Interpretation Act* (Ch. 2).

The interpretation of ordinary statutes is governed by section 3 of the *Interpretation Act* (Ch. 2), see *Ero Kolaip Puri v Jacob Kambily and Lagaip Local Government Council* (1998) N1776.

- refer to the *Interpretation Act No. 7 of 2005* (Autonomous Region of Bougainville)[173] as regards the statute law of the Autonomous Region of Bougainville.

- **Punctuation**

  The failure to take account of punctuation disregards the reality that literate people punctuate using grammatical principles and therefore, punctuation should be used in the interpretation of statutes.[174]

  Nevertheless, in order to achieve an interpretation according to the intention of the Parliament, punctuation may need to be ignored, therefore, applying the purposive rule.

  A comma is one means of expressing intention in a statutory provision, and a Court is entitled to have regard to it, though of course not to be controlled by it if the 'context' nevertheless requires otherwise.[175]

[3.0] EXTRINSIC AIDS

Extrinsic aids may be used in order to interpret a statutory provision.

The phrase 'extrinsic aids' refers to:

> any material that sheds light on the background to the enactment of a particular statute.[176]

---

[173] There however appears to be no legislative or constitutional authority for this statute to be enacted.

Irrespective, a provincial law that is inconsistent with a National law may be ruled to be unconstitutional, see *Re Forestry Act 1991 and the East New Britain Forestry Operations Control Act 1992* [1992] PNGLR 514, [1992] PGSC 6.

[174] See *Hanlon v The Law Society* [1981] AC 124; *Royal South Australian Yacht Squadron v Attorney-General* [1938] SASR 430 at 432 and *Davidson v Board of the Territory Insurance Office* (1981) 13 NTR 1.

[175] See *Committee of Direction of Fruit Marketing v Collins* (1925) 36 CLR 410, per Isaacs J at 421.

[176] See Report on Statutory Drafting and Interpretation: Plain Language and the Law [2000] IELRC 61, paragraph 5.03.

AIDS TO INTERPRETATION

Such aids include:

- **Historical Setting**[177]

  A Court may have regard to:

  - the history of the statute;

    and

  - the reasons that led to it being passed.[178]

  The purpose of a statute may be gathered from the historical context and background to the statute[179], including provisions that have been repealed.[180]

  By referring to the course of amendments it may be possible to more readily derive the policy that lies behind the provision in order to ascertain whether, even a strong presumption is rebutted. The permissibility of examining legislative history for this purpose is not in doubt.[181]

---

[177] See *K and S Lake City Freighters Pty Ltd v Gordon and Gotch Ltd* (1985) 157 CLR 309 at 315 and *Wik Peoples v Queensland* (1996) 187 CLR 1, per Gummow J at 171.

[178] See *Thomson v Lord Clanmorris* [1900] 1 Ch 718, per Lord Lindley MR at 725; *Read v Bishop of Lincoln* [1892] AC 644; *Edwards v Attorney General for Canada* [1930] AC 124 and *Schtraks v Government of Israel* [1964] AC 556 at 582-583.

See also: *Tse Moon-sak v Tse Hung and others* [1968] HKLR 159; *Po Fun-chan, Peter v Wong Hong-yuen, Peter* [1989] 2 HKLR 410 at 414 and *R v Leung Kam Ho* [1994] HKLD 48.

[179] See *Pambula District Hospital v Herriman* (1988) 14 NSWLR 387 at 410; *CIC Insurance Ltd v Bankstown Football Club Ltd* (1997) 187 CLR 384 at 408, [1997] HCA 2 and *Newcastle City Council v GIO General Ltd* (1997) 191 CLR 85 at 112, (1997) 149 ALR 623, (1997) 72 ALJR 97, [1997] HCA 53.

[180] See *Project Blue Sky Inc v Australian Broadcasting Authority* (1998) 194 CLR 355, per Brennan CJ at 366-368, [1998] HCA 28; *Palgo Holdings Pty Ltd v Gowans* (2005) 221 CLR 249 at 254; *R v Lavender* (2005) 222 CLR 67 at 81-85, [2005] HCA 37 and *R v Jennings* [1999] 1 VR 352.

[181] See *Ormond Investment Ltd v Betts* [1928] AC 143 at 156.

See also: *Mathieson v Burton* (1971) 124 CLR 1, [1971] HCA 4; *O'Grady v Northern Queensland Co Ltd* (1990) 169 CLR 356, per Brennan J at 365; *Hickling v Laneyrie* (1991) 21 NSWLR 730, per Kirby P at 736 and *Cafe Brandy Syndicate v Inland Revenue Commissioners* [1921] 2 KB 403.

AIDS TO INTERPRETATION

A Court may in limited circumstances examine a later statute to determine whether it throws any light upon the interpretation of an earlier statute.[182]

- **Hansard -- Parliamentary History and Debates**

Whilst hansard[183] may be used as an aid to the interpretation of legislation[184], it may not necessarily be illuminating by providing the vital clue to an intended meaning of a statutory provision[185].

---

[182] See *Cape Brandy Syndicate v Inland Revenue Commissioners* [1921] 2 KB 403, per Lord Sterndale at 414 and *Port of London Authority v Canvey Island Commissioners* [1932] 1 Ch 446, per Lawrence LJ at 493.

See also: *Deputy Federal Commissioner of Taxes (South Australia) v Elder's Trustee and Executor Co Ltd* (1936) 57 CLR 610 at 625-626, [1936] HCA 64; *Allina Pty Ltd v Commissioner of Taxation* (1991) 28 FCR 203 at 212; *Khoury v Government Insurance Office of New South Wales* (1984) 165 CLR 622, [1984] HCA 55 and *Commissioner of State Revenue (Victoria) v Pioneer Concrete (Victoria) Pty Ltd* (2002) 209 CLR 651, [2002] HCA 43.

See however: *Kirkness v John Hudson and Co* [1955] AC 696.

[183] Hansard which is kept in bound volumes is the written record of everything said in Parliament, including the First, Second and Third Readings.

[184] See *Graeme Rundle v Motor Vehicles Insurance (PNG) Trust* [1987] PNGLR 44 at 47; *The State v Danny Sunu and others* [1983] PNGLR 396 at 404 and *Rundle v Motor Vehicles Insurance (PNG) Trust (No. 1)* [1988-89] PNGLR 20.

See also: *Re Mew and Thorne* (1861) 31 LJBcy 87, (1862) 31 LJQB 201; *R v Bishop of Oxford* [1879] 4 QBD 525 at 550; *Pepper (Inspector of Taxes) v Hart* [1993] AC 593, per Lord Browne-Wilkinson at 634, [1992] 3 WLR 1032, [1993] 1 All ER 42; *Municipal Council of Sydney v Commonwealth* (1904) 1 CLR 208, per Griffiths CJ at 213-214; *Solomon Breweries Ltd v The Commissioner of Inland Revenue* [2003] SBHC 129; *United States of the American Trucking Association* (1940) 310 US 530 at 543-544; *In the Matter of National Irish Bank* [1999] 1 ILRM 321; *Pickstone v Freemans Plc* [1988] 2 All ER 803; *Stubbings v Webb* [1993] 2 WLR 120; *Chief Adjudication v Foster* [1993] 2 WLR 292, at 304-305; *R v Warwickshire CC; ex parte Johnson* [1993] 2 WLR 1 at 7; *Massmould Holdings v Payne* [1993] STC 62 at 74; *Scher v Policyholders Protection Board (No. 2)* [1993] 4 All ER 840 at 852; *Wacando v Commonwealth of Australia* (1981) 37 ALR 317, per Mason J at 335-336; *Federal Commissioner of Taxation v Whitfords Beach Pty Ltd* (1982) 39 ALR 521, per Mason J at 533-534; *TCN Channel Nine Pty Ltd v Australian Mutual Provident Society* (1982) 42 ALR 496 at 508 and *New Zealand Maori Council v Attorney-General* [1987] 1 NZLR 641.

[185] See *Pepper (Inspector of Taxes) v Hart* [1993] AC 593, per Lord Bridge at 617, [1992] 3 WLR 1032, [1993] 1 All ER 42.

However, there is the issue of relevance and Courts should discourage constant references to Hansard and indirect arguments, unless it is of obvious and direct importance.[186]

- **Second Reading Speech**

  Whilst the statements made by the Minister during the course of a Second Reading Speech may be used as an aid to interpretation, the words of a Minister should not be substituted for the words of the statute.[187]

  But even when that condition is met, it is for the Court when determining what was the intention of Parliament in using the words in question, to decide how much importance, or weight, if any, should be attached to such a statement.[188]

  Furthermore, the following conditions should be met before such statements are referred to as an aid to interpretation for the purpose of ascertaining the meaning of the statutory provision:

  - the legislation is ambiguous, obscure or leads to an absurdity;

  - the material relied upon consists of one or more statements by a Minister or other promoter of the Bill together if necessary with such other Parliamentary material as is necessary to understand such statements and their effect;

    and

  - the statements relied upon are clear.[189]

---

[186] See *Attorney-General v Whangarei City Council* [1987] 2 NZLR 150 at 152.

[187] See *Re Bolton; ex parte Douglas Beane* (1987) 162 CLR 514 at 518, [1987] HCA 12.

[188] See *R v Secretary of State for the Environment, Transport and the Regions; ex parte Spath Holme Ltd* [2001] 1 All ER 195, [2001] 2 WLR 15.

[189] See *Pepper (Inspector of Taxes) v Hart* [1993] AC 593, [1992] 3 WLR 1032, [1993] 1 All ER 42.

See also: *Commissioner of Rating and Valuation v Agrila Ltd* (2001) 4 HKCFAR 83 at 104; *Registrar of Births and Deaths v Syed Haider Yahya Hussain* (2001) 4 HKCFAR 429 at 444; *R v Environment Secretary; ex parte Spath Holme Ltd* [2001] 2 AC 349 at 392, 408 and 413 and *Robinson v Secretary of State* [2002] NI 390 at 405.

Subject to those conditions being met the Minister's statements may be used to resolve the ambiguity, obscurity or absurdity.[190]

- **Report of a Parliamentary Committee, Law Reform Commission and similar bodies**

  Where the legislation in question implements the recommendations of a report, such as a report of a Parliamentary Committee[191], Law Reform Commission[192] and similar bodies[193], the report may be used in order to identify the purpose of the legislation, provided there is ambiguity[194].

  A Court should however firstly construe the report and if the statute appears to depart from the recommendations of the report, it should then decide whether Parliament intended to act on or to depart from the recommendations.[195]

---

[190] See *HKSAR v Cheung Kwun Yin* [2009] HKCFA 66.

[191] See *Eastman Photographic Materials Co Ltd v Comptroller-General of Patents, Designs and Trade Marks* [1898] AC 571, per Lord Halsbury at 575; *Govindan Sellappah Nayar Kodakan Pillai v Punchi Banda Mundanayake* [1953] AC 514 at 528; *Letang v Cooper* [1965] 1 QB 232 and *Cozens v North Devon Hospital Management Committee and Hunter v Turners (Soham) Ltd* [1966] 2 WLR 1134.

See also: *Fothergill v Monarch Airlines Ltd* [1981] AC 251, per Lord Diplock at 281, [1980] 3 WLR 209; *Totalisator Agency Board v Wagner Cayley* [1963] WAR 180 and *Wacol Developments Pty Ltd v Realty Developments Pty Ltd* (1978) 140 CLR 503.

[192] See *Re Mew and Thorne* (1861) 31 LJBcy 87, (1862) 31 LJQB 201.

See also: *Fothergill v Monarch Airlines Ltd* [1981] AC 251, per Lord Diplock at 281, [1980] 3 WLR 209; *Whitely v Minister for Defence* [1997] 2 ILRM 416; *R v Secretary of State for Transport; ex parte Factortame Ltd* [1990] 2 AC 85; *Aswan Engineering v Lupdine Ltd* [1987] 1 WLR 1 at 14; *R v Allen* [1985] 1 AC 1029; *Fung Sang Trading Ltdv Kai Sun Sea Products and Food Co. Ltd* [1992] 1 HKLR 40; *Davis v Johnson* [1979] AC 264 and *Factortame Ltd and others v Secretary of State for Transport* [1990] 2 AC 85.

[193] See *Maher v Attorney-General* [1973] IR 140; *Comdel Ltd v Siporex S.A. (No. 2)* [1991] 1 AC 148; *Moran v Lloyd's* [1983] 1 QB 542 at 548; *Duke v Reliance Systems Ltd* [1988] 2 WLR 359; *Attorney General's Reference (No. 1 of 1988)* [1989] 1 AC 971 and *Re Conso Electronics (Far East) Ltd (In Liquidation)* [1995] 2 HKC 327.

[194] See *Salomon v Commissioners of Customs and Excise* [1967] 2 QB 116.

See also: *Comdel Ltd v Siporex S.A. (No. 2)* [1991] 1 AC 148 and *Barratt Scotland v Keith* [1993] SCLR 120.

[195] As commented by Ormrod J in *Firman v Ellis* [1978] 2 All ER 851, at 864.

More weight should be given to reports that contain recommendations and a draft Bill when there is no difference or material difference with the language of the statute.[196]

Such extrinsic aids should not be used to interpret a statutory provision, unless the interpretation of the provision suggested by that material is one that is reasonably open.[197]

If such an extrinsic aid suggests a different intention it would be necessary for the Court to reconsider whether the statute is really clear on the point because such an extrinsic aid should not override a statute.[198]

A Court cannot take an expression of intention from such extrinsic aids to supply an omission by the draftsperson when the result cannot reasonably be deduced from the words actually used by a recognised technique of statutory interpretation.[199]

- **International Conventions and Treaties**

Provided that there is cogent extrinsic evidence that a statute was intended to implement the government's obligations under an international convention or treaty, then the Court may look at the international convention or treaty[200] when interpreting the statute even though the statute does not mention it.[201]

---

[196] As commented by Viscount Dilhorne in *Black-Clawson International Ltd v Papierwerke Waldhof-Aschaffenburg Attorney-General* [1975] AC 591 at 622-623.

[197] See *Newcastle City Council v GIO General Ltd* (1997) 191 CLR 85, per McHugh J at 113, (1997) 149 ALR 623, (1997) 72 ALJR 97, [1997] HCA 53.

[198] See *Brown v Langwoods Photo Stores Ltd* [1991] 1 NZLR 173 at 176.

[199] See *Wentworth Securities Ltd v Jones* [1980] AC 74 and *Cooper Brookes (Wollongong) Pty Ltd v Federal Commissioner of Taxation* (1981) 147 CLR 297.

[200] It does not matter whether the international convention or treaty is in a foreign language, see *James Buchanan and Co Ltd v Babco Forwarding and Shipping (United Kingdom) Ltd* [1978] AC 141 at 152; *Corocraft Ltd v Pan American Airways Inc* [1969] 1 QB 616; *Fothergill v Monarch Airlines Ltd* [1981] AC 251, [1980] 3 WLR 209 and *Hill and Delamain (Hong Kong) Ltd v Manohar Gangaram Ahuia* [1994] 1 HKLR 353 at 362.

[201] See *Salomon v Commissioners of Customs and Excise* [1967] 2 QB 116 and *Post Office v Estuary Radio Ltd* [1968] 2 QB 74.

See also: *Winfat Enterprises (Hong Kong) Co Ltd v Attorney General* [1984] HKLR 32; *Fothergill v Monarch Airlines Ltd* [1981] AC 251, [1980] 3 WLR 209 and *Buchanan and Co v Babco Ltd* [1978] AC 141 at 152.

But the words of an international convention or treaty should not control or influence the meaning of a statutory provision, unless it appears that the statute was intended to give effect to the international convention or treaty, in which event a Court may resort to the international convention or treaty in order to resolve any ambiguity.[202]

The words of the statute should be interpreted by a Court as being intended to carry out the State's international convention and treaty obligations, and not in any manner inconsistent therewith, provided the words of the statute are reasonably capable of bearing such meaning.[203]

If the words of a statute are not clear, but are reasonably capable of more than one meaning, then the interpretation that is consonant with the international convention or treaty obligations is to be preferred. Such an interpretation will accord with the *prima facie* presumption that Parliament does not intend to act in breach of international law, including specific convention or treaty obligations.[204]

However, if the relevant statutory provisions are clear then such provisions must be given effect to, whether or not the statute complies with the relevant convention or treaty obligations.[205]

---

[202] See *Salomon v Commissioners of Customs and Excise* [1967] 2 QB 116 and *Post Office v Estuary Radio Ltd* [1968] 2 QB 74.

See also: *Winfat Enterprises (Hong Kong) Co Ltd v Attorney General* [1984] HKLR 32; *Fothergill v Monarch Airlines Ltd* [1981] AC 251, [1980] 3 WLR 209; *Buchanan and Co v Babco Ltd* [1978] AC 141 at 152; *Yager v R* (1977) 139 CLR 28, per Mason CJ at 43-44 and *Kruger v The Commonwealth* (1997) 190 CLR 1, per Dawson J at 71.

[203] See *Garland v British Rail Engineering Ltd* [1983] 2 AC 751, per Lord Diplock at 771; *Chu Kheng Lim v Minister for Immigration Local Government and Ethnic Affairs* (1992) 176 CLR 1 at 38 and *Minister for Immigration and Ethnic Affairs v Teoh* (1995) 183 CLR 273 at 287.

See also: *Bourke v Attorney General* [1972] IR 36.

A treaty should be interpreted in accordance with the ordinary meaning of its words and in the light of its object and purpose, so as to achieve its object or purpose, see *Applicant A v Minister for Immigration and Ethnic Affairs* (1996-1997) 190 CLR 225.

[204] See *Garland v British Rail Engineering Ltd* [1983] 2 AC 751.

[205] See *Ellerman Lines Ltd v Murray* [1931] AC 126 at 144

- **Overseas Statute**

  When a statutory provision is modeled on a corresponding provision in the statute of another country a Court may refer to that other statute in order to assist in statutory interpretation.[206]

- **Background Provided by other legislation**[207]

- **Re-enactment**

  There is a presumption[208] that where a word or phrase of doubtful meaning has received a clear judicial interpretation, the subsequent statute that incorporates the same word or phrase in a similar context should be construed so that the word or phrase is interpreted according to the meaning that has previously been assigned to it.[209]

- **Acts in Pari Materia**

  There is a common law maxim to the effect that statutes can be construed together when they are 'in pari materia'.[210]

  Statutes are 'in pari materia' when they deal with the same subject matter[211], ie., same person, thing or class as the one being dealt with[212].

---

[206] See *Director of Public Prosecutions v McDonagh* [1996] 2 ILRM 468.

[207] See *Toronto Suburban Railway Co v Toronto Corporation* [1915] AC 590 at 597.

[208] See *R v Chard* [1983] 3 WLR 835.

[209] See *Barras v Aberdeen Steam Trawling and Fishing Co* [1933] AC 402, per Lord Buckmaster at 411.

[210] See Report on Statutory Drafting and Interpretation: Plain Language and the Law [2000] IELRC 61, paragraph 5.28.

[211] See Report on Statutory Drafting and Interpretation: Plain Language and the Law [2000] IELRC 61, paragraph 5.28.

[212] See The Law Reform Commission of Hong Kong, 1997, 'Report on Extrinsic Materials as an Aid to Statutory Interpretation', March, page 30.

A presumption then arises that the legislature intended words and concepts which are common to these related statutes to have the same meaning in each.[213]

Statutes that are 'in pari materia' are to be taken together as forming one system and as interpreting and enforcing each other[214], even though the different statutes were enacted at different times and even expired and not referring to each other[215].

However, earlier Acts 'in pari materia' should only be used as an aid in interpretation where there is an ambiguity.[216]

Where a word or expression in a statute has received a clear judicial interpretation, there is a presumption that the subsequent statute that incorporates the same word or expression in a similar context should be construed so that the word or expression is interpreted according to the meaning that has previously been ascribed to it, unless a contrary intention appears.[217]

A statute is 'in pari materia' if it:

- expressly is;

  or

- impliedly should be

read with another statute.

The context in which a statute is to be interpreted includes other statutes 'in pari materia'.[218]

---

[213] See Report on Statutory Drafting and Interpretation: Plain Language and the Law [2000] IELRC 61, paragraph 5.28.

[214] See *R v Holland Palmer* [1785] 1 Leach 352 at 355.

See also: *Murphy v Dublin Corporation* [1976] IR 143 and *Irish Agricultural Machinery Ltd v O'Culacháin* [1990] 1 IR 535.

[215] See *R v Loxdale* [1758] 1 Burr 445 at 447.

[216] See *R v Titterton* [1895] 2 QB 61 at 67.

[217] See *Cronin v Youghal Carpets (Yarns) Ltd* [1985] IR 312 at 321.

[218] See *The Medical Council of Hong Kong v David Chow Siu Shek* [2000] HKCFA 58, [2000] 3 HKCFAR 144, [2000] 2 HKLRD 674.

Some statutory provisions that are read expressly 'in pari materia' with other statutes are as follows:

- the *Interpretation Act* (Ch. 2) is an Act which is read expressly 'in pari materia' with all other Acts[219];

- section 48A of the *Summary Offences Act* (Ch. 264) states:

  'Sections 363 to 373 of the *Criminal Code* apply to offender under this Division [Part V of Division 2]';

- section 22 of the *Criminal Code* (Ch. 262) states:

  'This Division [Division 5 – Criminal Responsibility] applies to all persons charged with offences against any law';

- section 1 of the *Motor Traffic Act* (Ch. 243) states that the term 'drug' is defined as:

  'a dangerous drug within the meaning of the *Dangerous Drugs Act*';

- section 2 of the *Search Act* (Ch. 341) states:

  that the *Search Act* (Ch. 341) applies notwithstanding the provisions of any other law, to and in relation to any search whether by or under that Act or any other law, other than a search carried out under a warrant issued under the *National Intelligence Organisation Act 1984* or a search carried out under the *Civil Aviation Act 2000*;

  and

- section 23 of the *Arrest Act* (Ch. 339) states:

  that the 'provisions of that Act which specify the circumstances in which a person may be arrested are in addition to and not in derogation of a provision of any other Act or subordinate enactment which confers a power of arrest'.

---

[219] See section 2.

Statutes may also be impliedly[220] read 'in pari materia' when there is no express statutory provision.[221]

The defence of 'provocation'[222] has been held to apply to the offence of 'Assault' as provided for by section 6 of the *Summary Offences Act* (Ch. 264).[223]

- **Textbook**[224]

- **Respected Dictionary**

A respected dictionary may be used as an aid in the interpretation of a statutory provision[225] with caution[226] in order to determine the ordinary and natural meaning of a word or phrase, 'unless a preposterous or unjust result would eventuate'[227].

---

220 See also: *Wui-Wapi and seventeen others v Ludwick Kembu* [1984] PNGLR 7; *Constitutional Reference No. 3 of 1978* [1978] PNGLR 421; *Agiru Aieni and twelve others v Paul T Tahain* [1978] PNGLR 37 and *Maxwell Arthur Schliebs v H Singh* [1981] PNGLR 364 at 369.

221 See *R v Loxdale* [1758] 1 Burr 445, per Lord Mansfield at 447.

See also: *Rainey v Greater Glasgow Health Board* [1987] AC 224 at 240.

222 See section 267 of the *Criminal Code* (Ch. 262).

223 See *SCR No. 6 of 1984; Re Provocation* [1985] PNGLR 31, [1985] PGSC 21.

224 See *Bastin v Davies* [1950] 2 KB 579 and *Letang v Cooper* [1965] 1 QB 232 at 240.

See also: *Fothergill v Monarch Airlines Ltd* [1981] AC 251, [1980] 3 WLR 209.

225 See *Madang Timbers Ltd v Valentive Kambori and others* (2009) SC992; *Dr Allan Kulunga and Western Highlands Provincial Government and others* (2006) SC859 and *Gini v University of Technology and Pearce New Guinea University of Technology and Independent State of Papua New Guinea* [1991] PNGLR 201 at 204.

See also: *Stone v Ross; ex parte Stone* [1976] Qd R 219; *Falconer v Pederson* [1974] VR 185 at 185-189; *Hardwick Game Farm v Suffolk Agricultural Poultry Producers Association* [1966] 1 WLR 287; *Re State of Norway's Application* [1989] 2 WLR 458; *Fothergill v Monarch Airlines Ltd* [1981] AC 251, [1980] 3 WLR 209 and *R v Peters* [1886] 16 QBD 636, per Lord Coleridge at 641.

226 See *Wau Ecology Institution and others v Registrar of Companies and others* (2005) SC794 and *The State v Alan Bekau* [1982] PNGLR 119.

227 See *SCR No. 2 of 1982; Re Kunangel* [1991] PNGLR 1 and *Ben Wafia and others v The State* (2006) SC851.

However, a dictionary should only be used as an aid in the interpretation in the absence of any judicial guidance or authority.[228]

- **Subordinate Legislative Enactment**[229]

  A Court should not interpret a statute by reference to a subordinate legislative enactment that was made under it.[230]

  However, a subordinate legislative enactment may be looked at to confirm the interpretation that a Court considers the legislation properly bears.[231]

Notwithstanding the use of extrinsic material as an aid to interpretation the search for meaning in a statute must always begin with the text of the relevant provisions.[232]

---

[228] See *Kerr v Kennedy* [1942] 1 KB 409, per Asquith J at 413.

[229] Refer also to the chapter titled 'Subordinate Legislative Enactments'.

[230] See *Matu Mining Pty Ltd v Philemon Embel (Attorney-General) and Kare Puga Development Corporation Pty Ltd* (1995) SC483.

See also: *The Great Fingall Consolidated Ltd v Sheehan* (1905) 3 CLR 176, per Griffith CJ at 184, [1905] HCA 43; *Australian Coarse Grains Pool Pty Ltd v Barley Marketing Board* (1985) 157 CLR 605, per Mason J at 625, [1985] HCA 38; *Hunter Resources Ltd v Melville* (1988) 164 CLR 234, per Mason CJ and Gaudron J at 244, [1988] HCA 5; *Master Education Services Pty Ltd v Ketchell* (2008) 236 CLR 101 at 112, [2008] HCA 38; *Wallaby Grip Limited v QBE Insurance (Australia) Limited; Stewart v QBE Insurance (Australia) Limited* [2010] HCA 9; *Jackson v Hall* [1980] AC 854; *Webster v McIntosh* (1980) 49 FLR 317, per Brennan J at 321; *Thorn EMI Pty Ltd v Federal Commissioner of Taxation* (1987) 13 FCR 491, per Beaumont J at 498 and *Cassidy v Murray* (1995) 124 FLR 267 at 279-280.

See however: *BACTA v Westminster City Council* [1988] 1 All ER 740 at 745.

[231] See *Matu Mining Pty Ltd v Philemon Embel (Attorney-General) and Kare Puga Development Corporation Pty Ltd* (1995) SC483.

See also: *Hales v Bolton Leathers Ltd* [1951] AC 531, per Lord Normand at 544 and Lord Oaksey at 548.

[232] See *Roy Morgan Research Centre Pty Ltd v Commissioner for State Revenue (Victoria)* (2001) 207 CLR 72 at 77 and *Stevens v Kabushiki Kaisha Sony Computer Entertainment* (2005) 224 CLR 193 at 206 and 240-241, [2005] HCA 58.

Refer also to: Speech by The Honorable Justice Susan Crennan AC, Justice of the High Court of Australia, 'Statutes and the Contemporary Search for Meaning', Statute Law Society, London, UK, 2010.

MEANING OF WORDS AND PHRASES

[1.0] STATUTORY PROVISION

Section 23 of the *Underlying Act 2000* states:

> '(1) When interpreting any provision of, or any word, expression or proposition in any written law, the court shall give effect to any relevant customary practice, usage or perception recognised by the people to be affected as a result of the interpretation.
>
> (2) Subject to Subsection (1), when interpreting any provision of or any word, expression or proposition in any written law, the courts may consider how the courts in foreign jurisdictions have interpreted similar or identical provisions, words, expressions or propositions'.

[2.0] GENERAL PRINCIPLES

Words and phrases of the English language have an extraordinary range of meaning.[233]

The meaning attributed to individual words in a phrase ultimately dictates the interpretation that a Court gives to the phrase when taken as a whole.[234]

Therefore, when interpreting a statutory provision a Court should attempt to give meaning to every word.[235]

The question whether a word or phrase in a statute is to be given:

- its ordinary and natural meaning;
- some technical meaning;

  or
- some other meaning

---

233 See *Stock v Frank Jones (Tipton) Ltd* [1978] 1 WLR 231 at 236, [1978] 1 All ER 948.

234 See *Collector of Customs v Agfa-Gevaert Ltd* (1996) 186 CLR 389, (1996) 141 ALR 59, (1996) 71 ALJR 123, [1996] HCA 36.

Refer also to the chapter titled 'Read In Context'.

235 See *Project Blue Sky v Australian Broadcasting Authority* (1998) 194 CLR 355, [1998] HCA 28.

is a question of law.[236]

Whilst general words do not necessarily have an ordinary and natural meaning[237] a Court may take 'judicial notice[238]' of the meaning of such words.[239]

There is a presumption that where language of a statute has received judicial interpretation and Parliament again employs the same language in a subsequent statute, that Parliament intended the relevant language to be given the meaning which has been judicially attributed to it.[240]

Unless the meaning of the word or phrase is defined:

- by a statutory provision;

  or

- by the judgment of a Court

their ordinary and natural meaning is to be used[241], unless such a meaning leads to a preposterous or unjust result eventuating.[242]

---

236 See *Brutus v Cozens* [1973] AC 854, [1972] UKHL 6.

See also: *Pearlman v Keepers and Governors of Harrow School* [1979] QB 56, per Lord Denning MR at 67; *Jedko Game Co Pty Ltd v Collector of Customs (New South Wales)* (1987) 12 ALD 491 and *Collector of Customs v Pozzolanic Enterprises Pty Ltd* (1993) 43 FCR 280 at 287-288.

237 See *Maunsell v Olins* [1975] AC 373, per Lord Wilberforce at 385-386, [1974] 3 WLR 835.

238 Refer also to the section titled 'Judicial Notice' in the chapter titled 'Court Procedure' in the text titled 'Injia on Criminal Practice and Procedure in Papua New Guinea and the Pacific'.

239 See *Bendixen v Coleman* (1943) 68 CLR 451.

240 See *Salvation Army Property Trust v Shire of Ferntree Gulley* (1952) 85 CLR 159 at 174, [1952] HCA 4.

241 See *Royale Thompson and others v Canisius Karingu* (2008) SC954; *PLAR No. 1 of 1980; Request by Principal Legal Advisor on a Point of Law arising in a case where a person tried upon indictment has been acquitted* [1980] PNGLR 326, [1980] PGSC 15; *SCR No. 2 of 1995; Reference by Western Highlands Provincial Executive* (1995) SC486; *Paru Aihi v Sir Moi Avei (No. 2)* (2003) SC720 and *Hilary Singat v Commissioner of Police* (2008) SC910.

242 See *SCR No. 2 of 1982; Re Kunangel* [1991] PNGLR 1 and *Ben Wafia and others v The State* (2006) SC851.

MEANING OF WORDS AND PHRASES

The meaning of a technical legal term is a question of law.[243]

Evidence as to any technical or trade meaning of a word is admissible, provided that the word had been used in such a sense. Otherwise, it should have been interpreted in accordance with its ordinary and natural meaning.[244]

The question whether the facts of the case fall within a statutory provision as interpreted is generally a question of law.[245]

When determining the meaning of a 'word' or 'phrase' in a statutory provision the following procedure should be followed:

1. Refer to the 'Interpretation' section/s in the statute in question.

The purpose of a definition in a statute is to limit or modify the ordinary and natural meaning of a word.[246]

Therefore, when particular words or phrases the subject of a definition section are found in a statute such words and phrases are to be understood in the defined sense.[247]

2. Refer to section 3(1) of the *Interpretation Act* (Ch. 2)[248].

That section provides the definitions of a number of words and phrases and commences with the words:

> 'In any statutory provision'.

---

[243] See *Australian Gas Light Co v Valuer-General* (1940) 40 SR (NSW) 126 at 137-138; *Lombardo v Commissioner of Taxation (Commonwealth of Australia)* (1979) 40 FLR 208 at 215 and *Collector of Customs v Pozzolanic Enterprises Pty Ltd* (1993) 43 FCR 280 at 287-288.

[244] See *Pepsi Seven-Up Bottlers v Commissioner of Taxation* (1995) 62 FCR 289, per Hill J at 297 and *Federal Commissioner of Taxation v Hamersley Iron Pty Ltd* (1980) 33 ALR 251, per Gobbo J at 271-273.

[245] See *Hope v Bathurst City Council* (1980) 144 CLR 1 at 7; *Collector of Customs v Pozzolanic Enterprises Pty Ltd* (1993) 43 FCR 280 at 287-288 and *Life Insurance Co of Australia Ltd v Phillips* (1925) 36 CLR 60 at 79.

[246] See *Brutus v Cozens* [1973] AC 854, [1972] UKHL 6.

[247] See *Gibb v Commissioner of Taxation* (1966) 118 CLR 628 at 634, [1967] ALR 527.

[248] An Interpretation Act sets out the working assumptions according to which legislation is framed by Parliament, and applied by the courts, see *Attorney-General (Queensland) v Australian Industrial Relations Commission* (2002) 213 CLR 485 at 492-493.

See also: *Floor v Davis* [1980] AC 695 at 708.

That section contains definitions of words and phrases that are deemed to apply in any other statutory provision.[249]

3. Refer to the *Interpretation Act No. 7 of 2005* (Autonomous Region of Bougainville)[250] as regards the statute law of the Autonomous Region of Bougainville.

4. Refer to any relevant Papua New Guinean case law that may have assigned a definition for the word or phrase in the statute in question.[251]

It should not be assumed that the meaning assigned to words and phrases in one statute by either the National Court or Supreme Court can be applied to other statutes with the same words or phrases, without caution.[252]

---

[249] See section 2 of the *Interpretation Act* (Ch. 2).

The interpretation of ordinary statutes is governed by section 3 of the *Interpretation Act* (Ch. 2), see *Ero Kolaip Puri v Jacob Kambily and Lagaip Local Government Council* (1998) N1776.

[250] There however appears to be no legislative or constitutional authority for this statute to be enacted.

Irrespective, a provincial law that is inconsistent with a National law may be ruled to be unconstitutional, see *Re Forestry Act 1991 and the East New Britain Forestry Operations Control Act 1992* [1992] PNGLR 514, [1992] PGSC 6.

[251] See *SCR No. 6 of 1984; Re Provocation* [1985] PNGLR 31, per Los J at 42, [1985] PGSC 21 and *Maxwell Arthur Schliebs v H Singh* [1981] PNGLR 364, per Miles J at 369.

See also: *The Geelong Harbour Trust Commissioner v Gibbs, Bright and Co* (1970) 122 CLR 504, per Barwick CJ at 514.

Refer also to:

- the chapter titled 'Read In Context'; and
- the law in relation to 'Acts in pari materia' in the section titled 'Extrinsic Aids' in the chapter titled 'Aids To Interpretation'.

[252] See however: *Dan Salmon Kakaraya v The Ombusman Commission of Papua New Guinea and The Independent State of Papua New Guinea* (2003) N2478.

5. Refer to a respected dictionary[253] with caution[254] in order to determine the ordinary and natural meaning of the word or phrase, 'unless a preposterous or unjust result would eventuate'[255].

Caution must always be observed when defining a phrase because the interpretation of separate words of a phrase may not result in achieving its correct meaning.[256]

6. Refer to overseas case law with caution, including a legal textbook, if necessary.[257]

A Court may have recourse to a decision of a court outside of the National Judicial System for their persuasive value.[258]

It is not permissible in statutory interpretation to look at differently constructed statutes in other jurisdictions and assume that such statutes necessarily provide a guide to the interpretation of legislation of Papua New Guinea that may well differ in some of its objects.[259]

---

[253] See *Madang Timbers Ltd v Valentive Kambori and others* (2009) SC992; *Dr Allan Kulunga and Western Highlands Provincial Government and others* (2006) SC859 and *Gini v University of Technology and Pearce New Guinea University of Technology and Independent State of Papua New Guinea* [1991] PNGLR 201 at 204.

See also: *Stone v Ross; ex parte Stone* [1976] Qd R 219; *Falconer v Pederson* [1974] VR 185 at 185-189 and *Hardwick Game Farm v Suffolk Agricultural Poultry Producers Association* [1966] 1 WLR 287.

[254] See *Wau Ecology Institution and others v Registrar of Companies and others* (2005) SC794 and *The State v Alan Bekau* [1982] PNGLR 119.

[255] See *SCR No. 2 of 1982; Re Kunangel* [1991] PNGLR 1 and *Ben Wafia and others v The State* (2006) SC851.

[256] See *Lee v The Showmen's Guild of Great Britain* [1952] 2 QB 329.

[257] See section 23(2) of the *Underlying Law Act 2000.*

[258] See Schedule 2.12 of the *Constitution of the Independent State of Papua New Guinea.*

[259] See *National Mutual Life Association of Australasia Ltd v Godrich* (1909) 10 CLR 1, per Griffith CJ at 13-14; *R v Lennard* [1984] 1 Qd R 1, per Macrossan J at 9; *Humphries v Smith; ex parte Smith* [1963] Qd R 67, per Stable J at 75 and *Smith v Commissioner of Corrective Services* [1978] 1 NSWLR 317, per Hutley JA at 325.

MEANING OF WORDS AND PHRASES

[3.0] CURRENT MEANING

The modern approach to statutory interpretation is to give words and phrases their current meaning, the so-called 'Act is Always Speaking' approach.[260]

The basic interpretative rule is:

- the presumption that legislation is always speaking from the present;

  and

- that each statute is to be viewed as a living part of the current legal system, and not limited by circumstances that were current at the time of its enactment.[261]

The words of a statute should normally be interpreted in accordance with their:

- ordinary;

- natural;

  and

- current

meaning.[262]

There is no inconsistency between:

- the rule that the language of the statute retains the meaning it had when enacted;

  and

---

[260] See *Birmingham City Council v Oakley* [2001] 1 All ER 385, per Lord Hoffman at 396; *Inspector of Taxes v Kiernan* [1981] IR 117; *Keane v An Bord Pleanála* [1997] 1 IR 184; *Universal Studios v Mulligan* [1998] 1 ILRM 438; *Mandarin Records v MCPS (Ireland) Ltd* [1999] 1 ILRM 154 and *IBM Corp v Computer Imports Ltd* [1989] 2 NZLR 395.

[261] See Report on Statutory Drafting and Interpretation: Plain Language and the Law [2000] IELRC 61, paragraph 3.02.

[262] See *Joyce v Grimshaw* (2001) 105 FCR 232 at 244; *Australian Competition and Consumer Commission v The Daniels Corporation International Pty Ltd* (2001) 108 FCR 123 at 143-144 and *Daniels Corporation International Pty Ltd v Australian Competition and Consumer Commission* (2002) 213 CLR 543 at 570-571.

- the rule that a statute 'is always speaking'.[263]

Considering that statutes are usually intended to operate for many years it would be most inconvenient if Courts could never rely in difficult cases on the current meaning of statutes. In cases where the problem arises it is a matter of interpretation:

- whether a Court must search for the historical or original meaning of a statute;

  or

- whether it is free to apply the current meaning of the statute to present day conditions.[264]

When a statute employs a concept that may change in content with advancing knowledge, technology or social standards, it should be interpreted as it would be currently understood.[265]

[4.0] CONSISTENT MEANING

The general rule is:

> where the same word or phrase appears at different places in a statute its meaning is presumed to be the same.[266]

---

[263] See *R (Quintavalle) v Secretary of State for Health* [2003] 2 AC 687, per Lord Bingham at 695.

[264] See *R v Ireland and R v Burstow* [1997] 4 All ER 225, [1998] AC 147, per Lord Steyne at 233 and 158-159.

[265] See *Birmingham City Council v Oakley* [2001] 1 All ER 385, per Lord Hoffman at 396.

[266] See *Slazengers (Australia) Pty Ltd v Burnett* [1951] AC 13 at 21 and *Ministry of Health v Fox* [1951] Ch 369.

See also: *Khan v Attorney-General and Island Enterprises Limited v Attorney-General* [1984] SILR 105; *Registrar of Titles (Western Australia) v Franzon* (1976) 50 ALJR 4 at 6; *McLeish v F T Eastment and Sons Pty Ltd* (1970) 71 SR (NSW) 178 at 180 and *Craig Williamson Pty Limited v Barrowcliff* [1915] VLR 450, per Hodges J at 452.

MEANING OF WORDS AND PHRASES

Whilst it may be assumed that Parliament does not make mistakes when enacting legislation[267], Parliament does occasionally make mistakes[268].

Where it is clear that a legal draftsperson has forgotten the definition in a particular place where the defined term occurs, a Court may need to give the term its ordinary and natural meaning.[269]

Although generally in construing a statute words should be given their ordinary and natural meaning, the 'context' may indicate that a word is intended to have another meaning.[270]

[5.0] MUST/SHALL

Generally when interpreting the word 'must' it is interpreted as:

- an imperative;

  or

- mandatory.[271]

In its present or future tense the word 'must' expresses command, obligation, duty, necessity and inevitability.[272]

In contrast, the word 'shall' is an equivocal word that can express either command or simple futurity.[273]

---

267 See *SCR No. 4 of 1985; Omaro Garo v The Police* [1985] PNGLR 320, per Kidu CJ at 322, [1985] PGSC 4; *SCR No. 5 of 1987; Central Banking (Foreign Exchange and Gold) Regulations (Ch. 138)* [1987] PNGLR 433, [1987] PGSC 4 and *The State v Francis Angosiwen (No. 2)* (2004) N2670.

See also: *Commissioner for Special Purposes of the Income Tax v Pemsel* [1891] AC 531, per Lord Halsbury LC at 549.

268 See *The State v Francis Angosiwen (No. 2)* (2004) N2670.

269 See *R v Lynsey* [1995] 2 Cr App R 667 at 672, [1995] 3 All ER 654.

270 See *Dekarube v Agieroudi* [1975] NRSC 2.

271 See *Kosovich v Mancini* (1982) 31 SASR 272 at 275-276.

272 See *International Union v Massey-Ferguson Industries Ltd* (1979) 94 DLR (3d) 743, per Reid J at 745-746.

273 See *International Union v Massey-Ferguson Industries Ltd* (1979) 94 DLR (3d) 743, per Reid J at 745-746.

However, like all words, its meaning has to be taken from its 'context'.[274]

Where the word 'shall' is used in a written law conferring a power, it is to be interpreted, unless the 'context' otherwise requires, to imply that the power must be exercised.[275]

[6.0] MAY/MAY NOT

Whilst it is accepted that the word 'may' denotes the exercise of discretionary power[276], there may be circumstances or situations in which that discretionary element is removed.[277]

The word 'may' has been interpreted as mandatory or imperative.[278]

In such cases, however, reference is usually made to the purpose of the legislation, the nature of the power and the 'context' in which the word is used.[279]

[7.0] MAY/SHALL

In exceptional circumstances the word 'shall' may need to be interpreted to mean 'may' or vica versa.[280]

---

274 See *Re Griffiths* [1991] 2 Qd R 29, per Bryne J at 33.

275 See *Re the Electoral Act 1965-1973*, [1969-1982] NLR 107, [1977] NRSC 4.

See also: *Julius v Bishop of Oxford* (1880) 5 App Cas 214 at 222-223.

276 See *South Australian Cold Stores Ltd v Electricity Trust of South Australia* (1965) 39 ALJR 332, per Owen J at 338.

277 See *Tindiwi, for and on behalf of Members of the Suspended Enga Provincial Government v Nilkare, Minister for Provincial Affairs and The State* [1984] PNGLR 191, [1981] PGSC 18.

See also: *Mobil Oil Australia Ltd v Kwaeria* [2001] SBHC 116.

See however: *R v Snow* (1915) 20 CLR 315 at 322 and 362 and *R v Cheng* (1999) 48 NSWLR 616, [1999] NSWCCA 374.

278 See *Feratalia v Attorney-General* [2002] SBHC 73 and *Leach v R* [2007] HCA 3.

279 See *Feratalia v Attorney-General* [2002] SBHC 73 and *Leach v R* [2007] HCA 3.

280 See *Tindiwi v Nilkare* [1984] PNGLR 191 and *Enforcement of Human Rights Pursuant to Constitution s 57; Application by Karingu* [1988-89] PNGLR 278.

MEANING OF WORDS AND PHRASES

[8.0] AND/OR

Wherever the conjunctive 'and' is used:

- all the matters or factors listed must all exist;

  or

- if it is a requirement, all of them must be met.[281]

Generally, words joined by 'and' are regarded as being 'cumulatives'; whereas words joined by 'or' (disjunctive) are regarded as 'alternatives', unless there is an obvious mistake when interpreting the legislation.

Therefore,

- if the word 'or' appears in a section as follows:

  '(a) [...];

  (b) [...]; or

  (c) [...]',

  the prima facie assumption is that the section will be satisfied if either subsections (a), (b) or (c) is satisfied;

  and

- if the word 'and' appears in a section as follows:

  '(a) [...];

  (b) [...]; and

  (c) [...]',

  the prima facie assumption is that the section will be satisfied only if all of the subsections are satisfied.

---

[281] See *SCR No. 5 of 1987; The Matter of the State v Songke Mai and Gai Avi Reference under s. 18 of the Constitution* [1988-89] PNGLR 56, Los J at 84, [1988] PGSC 22; *Sir Julius Chan v The Ombudsman Commission of Papua New Guinea* (1999) SC607 and *Rosa Angitai v The State* [1983] PNGLR 185 at 190.

See also: *Victims Compensation Fund Corporation v Brown* (2003) 7 ALJR 1797, [2003] HCA 54 and *Protective Commissioner v D* (2004) 60 NSWLR 513, [2004] NSWCA 216.

However, mistakes are recognised by the Courts[282] and statutes with mistakes are generally interpreted so as to rectify the mistake, thereby applying the 'purposive rule'. In such a circumstance the word 'and' may be interpreted as 'or'.[283]

Furthermore, a statute may specify that the word 'and' be interpreted as 'or'.

[9.0] IN PARTICULAR

The normal role of the phrase 'in particular' appearing after words describing a class of matters or matters of a general nature is:

> to identify a specific matter or specific matters which come within the general class or description.[284]

[10.0] NOTWITHSTANDING

The word 'notwithstanding' in common parlance means:

- in spite of;

  or

- irrespective.[285]

The inclusion of a 'notwithstanding phrase' in a statute is to mark and remove an obstacle to the intended legislation.[286]

---

[282] See *The State v Francis Angosiwen (No. 2)* (2004) N2670.

[283] See *Green v Premier Glynrhonwy State Co* [1928] 1 KB 561, per Sumner LJ at 568.

[284] See *Ricegrowers Co-Operative Mills Ltd v Bannerman* (1981) 56 FLR 443, per Bowen CJ and Franki J at 449.

[285] See *Keith Edward Garland Douglas v The Attorney-General* [2000] SBHC 9.

[286] See *Re Bread Carters (Cumberland) Board* [1922] AR (NSW) 73.

[11.0] NECESSARY

The word 'necessary' can have shades of meaning: it is not of 'a fixed character, peculiar to itself', but rather 'admits of all degrees of comparison'.[287]

Its meaning, therefore, depends on the 'context' in which it is used.[288]

[12.0] SUBJECT TO

The phrase 'subject to' is:

> a simple provision that merely subjects the provisions of one subject subsections to the provisions of the master subsections.[289]

Where there is no clash, the phrase does nothing.[290]

If there is a collision, the phrase shows what is to prevail.[291]

---

[287] See *McCulloch v Maryland* (1819) 17 US 159 at 203 and *Thomas v Mowbray* (2007) 233 CLR 307, [2007] HCA 33, per Gummow and Crennan JJ.

[288] See *Fairfax Digital Australia and New Zealand Pty Ltd v Ibrahim* [2012] NSWCCA 125.

Refer also to the chapter titled 'Read In Context'.

[289] See *C and J Clark Ltd v Inland Revenue Commissioner* [1973] 2 All ER 513, per Megarry J at 520 and *Smith v London Transport Executive* [1951] AC 555.

See also: *Pun Jong Sau v Poon Wing Kong* [1977-1979] HKC 210, per Trainor J at 219 and *Auditor-General v Attorney-General (representing the Accountant-General)* [2005] SBHC 30.

[290] See *Michael Ayakamp v Guringing B* [1981] PNGLR 531 at 533.

See also: *C and J Clark Ltd v Inland Revenue Commissioner* [1973] 2 All ER 513, per Megarry J at 520; *Smith v London Transport Executive* [1951] AC 555; *Pun Jong Sau v Poon Wing Kong* [1977-1979] HKC 210, per Trainor J at 219 and *Auditor-General v Attorney-General (representing the Accountant-General)* [2005] SBHC 30.

[291] See *Michael Ayakamp v Guringing B* [1981] PNGLR 531 at 533.

See also: *C and J Clark Ltd v Inland Revenue Commissioner* [1973] 2 All ER 513, per Megarry J at 520; *Smith v London Transport Executive* [1951] AC 555; *Pun Jong Sau v Poon Wing Kong* [1977-1979] HKC 210, per Trainor J at 219 and *Auditor-General v Attorney-General (representing the Accountant-General)* [2005] SBHC 30.

The phrase provides no warranty of universal collision.[292]

[13.0] DEEMED MEANING

[13.1] INTRODUCTION[293]

When a statute specifically defines the meaning of a word or phrase, it applies a 'deemed' meaning because such a word or phrase is deemed to have the meaning assigned.[294]

Therefore, the ordinary and natural meaning of such a word or phrase cannot be applied.

A deeming provision is a legal fiction and is used to:

> create an artificial construction of a word or phrase in a statute that would not otherwise prevail.[295]

The primary function of a deeming provision is:

> to bring in something that would otherwise be excluded.[296]

A deeming provision should be interpreted:

- strictly;

  and

- only for the purpose for which it was created

---

[292] See *C and J Clark Ltd v Inland Revenue Commissioner* [1973] 2 All ER 513, per Megarry J at 520 and *Smith v London Transport Executive* [1951] AC 555.

See also: *Pun Jong Sau v Poon Wing Kong* [1977-1979] HKC 210, per Trainor J at 219 and *Auditor-General v Attorney-General (representing the Accountant-General)* [2005] SBHC 30.

[293] See *Hunter Douglas Australia Pty Ltd v Perma Blinds* (1970) 122 CLR 49, per Windeyer J at 65-67, [1970] HCA 63; *The Council of the Shire of Redland v Stradbroke Rutile Pty Ltd* (1974) 133 CLR 641, per Gibbs J at 655, [1974] HCA 4 and *Macquarie Bank Ltd v Fociri Pty Ltd* (1992) 27 NSWLR 203 at 207.

[294] See for example, section 3 of the *Interpretation Act* (Ch. 2).

[295] See *Ex parte Walton, Re Levy* (1881) 17 ChD 746.

[296] See *Malaysia Building Society Bhd v Lim Kheng Kim and others* (1988) 3 MLJ 175.

and its application should not be extended.[297]

[13.2] MEANS

The interpretation of the word 'means' that is used in a 'deemed' definition has caused difficulties for the courts over the years.[298]

Clearly the word 'means' as regards a definition indicates an exhaustive definition, ie., the word or phrase has no other meaning.

[13.3] INCLUDES

The interpretation of the word 'includes' that is used in a 'deemed' definition has caused difficulties for the Courts over the years.[299]

The word 'includes' primarily has an expansive function.

Usually, a definition which states that a word includes specified matters reveals a Parliamentary intention to add the meanings given in the definition to the ordinary meaning of the word.

A function of an inclusive definition is:

> to extend the ordinary and natural meaning of the particular word or phrase to include matters that otherwise would not be encompassed by it.[300]

The ordinary meaning is amplified to the extent specified.[301]

---

[297] See *FCT v Comber* (1986) 64 ALR 451.

[298] See *MacFarlane v Burke; ex parte Burke* [1983] 2 Qd R 584, per Macrossan J at 595.

[299] See *MacFarlane v Burke; ex parte Burke* [1983] 2 Qd R 584, per Macrossan J at 595.

[300] See *Corporate Affairs Commission (South Australia) v Australian Central Credit Union* (1985) 157 CLR 201 at 206-207; *Buckle v Josephs* (1983) 47 ALR 787, per Toohey J at 792 and Lockhart J at 796; *Sherritt Gordon Mines Ltd v Federal Commissioner of Taxation* [1977] Vic Rp 42, [1977] VR 342, per McInerney J at 353-354 and *Re Gray; ex parte Marsh* (1985) 157 CLR 351 at 365.

[301] See *Sherritt Gordon Mines Ltd v Federal Commissioner of Taxation* [1977] Vic Rp 42, [1977] VR 342, per McInerney J at 353.

MEANING OF WORDS AND PHRASES

The word 'includes' is:

- a word of extension;

  and

- not of restrictive definition.[302]

A definition of the word 'includes' does not necessarily purport to be complete or exhaustive.[303]

However, whilst the word 'includes' is prima facie 'inclusive', it may be interpreted as 'exhaustive' depending on the 'context' of the statute in question.[304]

When considering that the word 'includes' denotes a legislative intention to enlarge the ordinary meaning of the word defined, unless perhaps the items included in the definition would fall within it. In that case the definition, though introduced by the word 'includes', might be regarded as exhaustive.[305]

It will more readily appear that the definition is not exhaustive where that which is included goes beyond the natural import of the word.[306]

However, prima facie a definition with the word 'includes' should not be considered as 'exhaustive' in meaning.[307]

---

[302] See *Hook v Rolfe* (1986) 7 NSWLR 40, per Samuels JA at 49-50.

[303] As observed by Coleridge LCJ in *R v Hermann* (1879) 4 QBD 284 at 288.

[304] See *Dilworth v Commissioner of Stamps* [1899] AC 99, per Lord Watson at 105.

See also: *YZ Finance Co Pty Ltd v Cummings* (1963) 109 CLR 395 at 399, 404 and 406, [1964] HCA 12.

[305] See *YZ Finance Co Pty Ltd v Cummings* (1964) 109 CLR 395, [1964] HCA 12 and *R v McN* [1963] SR (NSW) 186, (1963) 80 WN 608.

[306] See *MacFarlane v Burke; ex parte Burke* [1983] 2 Qd R 584.

[307] See *Robinson v Barton-Eccles Local Board* (1883) 8 App Cas 798, per Lord Selborne LC at 801.

See also: *R v Tkacz* (2001) 25 WAR 77, per Malcolm CJ, [2001] WASCA 391 and Statutory Interpretation in Australia, 2nd ed., 1981, pages 115-118.

[13.4] CLASS RULE

The 'ejusdem generis' or 'class rule', often known as the rule in Heydon's case[308], provides:

> where in a statute there are general words following particular and specific words, the general words must be confined to things of the same kind as those specified.[309]

For example, if a statute provides:

> 'The term "motor vehicle" includes motor cars, motor bikes and other vehicles',

by virtue of this rule of statutory interpretation, the words 'and other vehicles' would not apply to any other vehicle that did not have a motor.

However, this rule of statutory interpretation is not a rule of law[310] and must be applied with caution and as a guide[311], subject to the primary rule that:

> statutes are to be construed in accordance with the intention of Parliament.[312]

[13.5] WORDS OF INCLUSION AND EXCLUSION

Some definitions have both 'inclusionary' and 'exclusionary' elements.

For example, if a statute provides:

> 'The term "motor vehicle" includes motor cars, motor bikes and other vehicles, but does not include motor boats',

the 'words of exclusion' are 'but does not include motor boats'.

Therefore, a motor boat although it has a motor has been excluded from the definition of that term.

---

308 (1584) 3 Co. Rep. 7a.

309 See *Dean v Attorney-General of Queensland* [1971] Qd R 391, per Stable J at 403.

310 See *Cody v J H Nelson Pty Ltd* (1947) 74 CLR 629.

311 See *Cody v J H Nelson Pty Ltd* (1947) 74 CLR 629, per Dixon J at 649.

312 See *Dean v Attorney-General of Queensland* [1971] Qd R 391 and *Mattinson v Multiplo Incubators Pty Ltd* [1977] 1 NSWLR 368, per Mahoney JA at 375.

Such words may however not assist in the interpretation of such terms.[313]

[313] See *Corporate Affairs Commission v Australian Central Credit Union* (1985) 157 CLR 201, (1985) 61 ALR 236.

PENAL STATUTE

[1.0] GENERAL PRINCIPLES

A penal statute is a statute that includes an offence.[314]

A penal statute should be interpreted according to:

> its natural meaning without any presumption that it was intended to do no more than restate the existing law.[315]

When interpreting a penal statute a Court should be very careful not to place the liberty of a defendant in jeopardy, except where the Parliament has clearly so ruled.[316]

Whilst historically a rule of interpretation was that a penal statute must be construed strictly[317], the Courts are now less reluctant to place undue emphasis on this rule.[318]

---

[314] An act or omission in consequence of which a person may be imprisoned either immediately or upon non-payment of a fine is an offence, see *SCR No. 2 of 1989; Re Village Courts Act* (Ch 44) [1988-89] PNGLR 491, [1988] PGSC 30.

See also: *Public Employees Association of Papua New Guinea v Public Services Commission* [1983] PNGLR 206, [1983] PGSC 18, section 2 of the *Criminal Code* (Ch. 262) and section 3 of the *Interpretation Act* (Ch. 2).

However, no person shall be convicted of an offence on account of any act that did not, at the time when it took place, constitute an offence, see section 37(7) of the *Constitution of the Independent State of Papua New Guinea* and section 178 of the *Constitution of the Autonomous Region of Bougainville*.

[315] See *Brennan v R* (1936) 55 CLR 253 at 263.

[316] See *William Douglas McCluskey v The Attorney-General and others* [1993] SBHC 88.

[317] See *Baiza Tadu Avona v The State* [1986] PNGLR 148, [1986] PGSC 2; *SCR No. 6 of 1984; Re Provocation* [1985] PNGLR 31, per McDermott J at 35 and Amet J (as he then was) at 38, [1985] PGSC 21; *The State v Danny Sunu and others* [1983] PNGLR 396 at 407 and 414 and *SCR No. 1 of 1981; Re Inter-Group Fighting Act* [1981] PNGLR 151 at 154.

See also: *Kelsey v Hill* [1995] 1 Qd R 182; *Carrol v Mijovich* (1991) 58 A Crim R 243, per Handley LA at 257; *Murphy v Farmer* (1988) 165 CLR 19, per Deane, Dawson and Gaudron JJ at 28-29; *Waugh v Kippen* (1986) 160 CLR 156; *Davern v Messel* (1984) 155 CLR 21, per Gibbs CJ at 31; *Smith v Corrective Services Commission (New South Wales)* (1980) 147 CLR 134, per Stephen, Mason, Murphy, Aickin and Wilson JJ at 139 and *Tuck and Sons v Priester* [1887] QBD 629 at 638.

[318] See *Director of Public Prosecutions Reference (No. 1 of 1992); Director of Public Prosecutions Reference (No. 1 of 1993)* (1993) 65 A Crim R 197 and *R v Lavender* (2005) 222 CLR 67, [2005] HCA 37, per Kirby J.

PENAL STATUTE

The rule of statutory interpretation that words of a penal provision should be strictly adhered to is now considered to be a rule of last resort.[319]

In determining the meaning of a penal statute the ordinary rules of interpretation must be applied[320], but if the language of the statute remains ambiguous or doubtful the ambiguity or doubt may be resolved in favour of a defendant[321], ie., the principle of doubtful penalisation[322].

There should only be a strict interpretation of a penal statute or of a statute that affects the personal liberty of a person, such as the *Correctional Service Act 1995*[323], if there is ambiguity or doubt in its interpretation.[324]

A penal statute should not be interpreted so as to lead to unfairness.[325]

---

319 See *Beckwith v R* (1976) 135 CLR 569, per Gibbs J at 576, [1976] HCA 55 and *R v Lavender* (2005) 222 CLR 67, [2005] HCA 37, per Kirby J.

320 See *R v Chapman* [1931] 2 KB 606, per Hewart LCJ at 609; *Bowers v Gloucester Corporation* [1963] 1 QB 881, per Parker LCJ at 887 and *Director of Public Prosecutions v Ottewell* [1968] 3 WLR 621, per Lord Reid at 627.

See also: *R v Adams* (1935) 53 CLR 563 at 567-568, [1935] HCA 62; *Beckwith v R* (1976) 135 CLR 569, per Gibbs J at 576, [1976] HCA 55; *Lee Vanit v R* (1997) 72 ALJR 1, per Kirby J at 13, [1997] HCA 51 and *R v Paré* (1987) 38 CCC (3d) 97 at 106.

321 See *R v Sleep* [1966] Qd R 47 at 54; *Director of Public Prosecutions Reference (No. 1 of 1992); Director of Public Prosecutions Reference (No. 1 of 1993)* (1993) 65 A Crim R 197; *Deming No 456 Pty Ltd v Brisbane Unit Development Corporation Pty Ltd* (1983) 155 CLR 129 at 145; *Chew v R* (1992) 173 CLR 626 at 632 and 642 and *Kelsey v Hill* [1995] 1 Qd R 182 at 185.

322 See *Mullins v District Judge William Harnett* [1998] 2 ILRM 304.

323 See *Smith v Corrective Services Commission (New South Wales)* (1980) 147 CLR 134 at 139, [1980] HCA 49.

324 See *The State v James Tei Wena; The State v Gend Yanisa Thomas* (2000) N2304.

See also: *R v Chapman* [1931] 2 KB 606, per Hewart LCJ at 609; *Bowers v Gloucester Corporation* [1963] 1 QB 881, per Parker LCJ at 887; *Director of Public Prosecutions v Ottewell* [1968] 3 WLR 621, per Lord Reid at 627; *R v Adams* (1935) 53 CLR 563 at 567-568, [1935] HCA 62; *Beckwith v R* (1976) 135 CLR 569, per Gibbs J at 576, [1976] HCA 55; *Lee Vanit v R* (1997) 72 ALJR 1, per Kirby J at 13, [1997] HCA 51 and *R v Paré* (1987) 38 CCC (3d) 97 at 106.

325 See *Director of Public Prosecutions (Commonwealth of Australia) v WJB* [2000] SASC 364, per Prior J.

PENAL STATUTE

[2.0] CODES SPECIFICALLY[326]

[2.1] GENERAL PRINCIPLES

In *John Kasaipwalova v The State*[327] Kearney J, as a member of the Supreme Court, stated:

> 'The correct approach to the interpretation of a section of a code is that stated by Dixon and Evatt JJ in Brennan v The King (1936) 55 CLR 253 at p 263, as follows: "... it forms part of a code intended to replace the common law, and its language should be construed accordingly to its natural meaning and without any presumption that it was intended to do no more than restate the existing law. It is not the proper course to begin by finding how the law stood before the Code, and then see if the Code will bear an interpretation which will leave the law unaltered'. This passage does not mean that it is never necessary to resort to the common law for the purpose of aiding in the construction of the Code – it may be justifiable to turn back to the common law where the Code contains provisions of doubtful import, or uses language which had previously acquired a technical meaning, or some such special ground."'

Resort to the common law is appropriate only where the language of the Code:

- is ambiguous[328];
- has a technical or special meaning acquired at common law[329];
- if there is something missing which it is necessary for the common law to fill[330];

---

[326] As regards the other principles of interpretation relating to the interpretation of a Code, see *Charlie v R* [1999] HCA 23, per Kirby J and *Roberts v The State of Western Australia* [2007] WASCA 48.

[327] [1977] PNGLR 257 at 280.

See also: *Bank of England v Vagliano Brothers* [1891] AC 107; *Robinson v Canadian Pacific Railway Co* [1892] AC 481 at 487; *Vallance v R* (1961) 108 CLR 56; *Parker v R* (1997) 71 ALJR 598, per Kirby J at 620; *R v Barlow* (1997) 188 CLR 1, (1997) 71 ALJR 680, per McHugh J at 689 and Kirby J at 696; *Stuart v R* (1974) 134 CLR 426 at 437; *Mellifont v Attorney-General (Queensland)* (1991) 173 CLR 289 at 309; *R v JS* [2007] NSWCCA 272; *Sungravure Pty Ltd v Middle East Airlines Airliban S.A.L.* (1974) 134 CLR 1; *Lee v R* [2007] NSWCCA 71; *Kaporonovski v R* (1973) 133 CLR 209, per Gibbs J at 236; *Boughey v R* (1986) 161 CLR 10 and *Ward v R* [1972] WAR 36.

[328] See *R v Lockwood; ex parte Attorney-General* [1981] Qd R 209.

[329] See *R v Johnson* [1964] Qd R 1.

[330] See *Callaghan v R* (1952) 87 CLR 115 and *R v Scarth* [1945] St R Qd 38.

or

- employs words and phrases that are conventionally used to express a general common law principle[331], including decisions subsequent to the Code's enactment[332].

The meaning of the words and phrases to be found in a Code is controlled by the 'context' in which such words and phrases are found. But when the 'context' does not exclude the common law principles that particular words and phrases impliedly import, reference to those common law principles is both permissible and required.[333]

[2.2] CRIMINAL CODE

Section 1 of the *Criminal Code Act* (Ch. 262) states:

> '"the Code" means the Code of Criminal Law contained in the Schedule'.

Therefore, the *Criminal Code* is actually a schedule to the *Criminal Code Act* (Ch. 262).

Furthermore, section 2 of the *Criminal Code Act* (Ch. 262) states:

> 'The provisions contained in Schedule 1 are the law of Papua New Guinea with respect to the matters dealt with in that Schedule'.

Considering that many parts of the *Criminal Code* (Ch. 262) were novel, introducing fundamental changes to the pre-existing criminal law[334] it is a codifying Act[335], and therefore:

> it should be interpreted applying the rules of interpretation that apply to the interpretation of a Code.[336]

---

[331] See *Mamote-Kulang v R* (1964) 111 CLR 62 at 76.

[332] See *Murray v R* [1962] Tas SR 170 at 172-173 and 192; *R v Rau* [1972] Tas SR 59 at 71-72 and *R v Martyr* [1962] Qd R 398 at 413.

[333] See *Boughey v R* (1986) 161 CLR 10, per Brennan J at 30.

[334] See *Wamela v The State* [1982] PNGLR 269, [1982] PGSC 24 and *SCR No. 6 of 1984; Re Provocation* [1985] PNGLR 31, [1985] PGSC 21, per McDermott J.

[335] See *Bank of England v Vegliano Brothers* [1891] AC 107 at 144.

[336] See *R v Martyr* [1962] Qd R 398 at 413.

PENAL STATUTE

Whilst the Code primarily supplies its meaning there are circumstances in which reference to the antecedent common law is justifiable. One such circumstance is where the Code contains provisions that are ambiguous or of doubtful import.[337]

Where the strict interpretation of the *Criminal Code* (Ch. 262) would give rise to an anomalous and unjust situation, the Supreme Court can and should on the authority of the *Constitution of the Independent State of Papua New Guinea*, and in particular section 158, remedy it so as to do what Parliament would have done if they were so aware.[338]

Furthermore, the provisions of the *Criminal Code Act* (Ch. 262) are not read expressly 'in pari materia[339]' with other statutes, unless otherwise stated in the Code. The provisions of Division 5 of Part I of the *Criminal Code* (Ch. 262) however apply to all persons charged with any offences against any law.[340]

[2.3] BAIL ACT

The *Bail Act* (Ch. 340) is a complete Code dealing with interim judicial release.[341]

---

337 See *R v Patel; ex parte Attorney-General (Queensland)* [2011] QCA 81; *Stuart v R* (1974) 134 CLR 426, per Gibbs J at 437 and *R v Barlow* (1997) 188 CLR 1, per McHugh J at 19, (1997) 71 ALJR 680.

338 See *PLAR No. 1 of 1980; Request by Principal Legal Adviser on a Point of Law arising in a case where a person tried under Indictment has been acquitted* [1980] PNGLR 326, [1980] PGSC 15 and *SCR No. 6 of 1984; Re Provocation* [1985] PNGLR 31, [1985] PGSC 21.

339 Refer also to the law in relation to 'Acts in Pari Materia' in the section titled 'Extrinsic Aids' in the chapter titled 'Aids To Interpretation'.

340 See section 22 of the *Criminal Code* (Ch. 262).

341 See *Re Herman Kagl Diawo* [1980] PNGLR 148, per Kearney DepCJ at 151, [1980] PGSC 9.

AMENDMENTS

[1.0] STATUTORY PROVISION

Section 55 of the *Interpretation Act* (Ch. 2) states:

> 'A statutory provision that amends another statutory provision shall, unless the contrary intention appears, be construed with and as part of the amended provision'.

[2.0] GENERAL PRINCIPLES

The meaning of the term 'amend' is:

> to alter the legal meaning of an Act or statutory provision, short of entirely rescinding it.[342]

Whether a statutory provision has been:

- amended;

  or

- repealed[343]

is always a matter of substance.[344]

When a statutory provision is repealed and re-enacted in a form which enlarges its scope, this has been interpreted as amounting in substance to an amendment because the new provision has been regarded as intended to be:

- retrospective so far as it is mere repetition'

  and

---

[342] See *Attorney-General (Western Australia) v Marquet* (2003) 217 CLR 545.

[343] Refer also to the chapter titled 'Repeals'.

[344] See *The State v Kaupa Kokia* (2005) N3012, [2005] PGNC 16.

See also: *Attorney-General (Western Australia) v Marquet* (2003) 217 CLR 545 and *Beaument v Yeomans* (1934) 3 SR (NSW) 562 at 569-570.

- prospective so far as it is new.[345]

The *Criminal Code (Sexual Offences and Crimes Against Children) Act 2002* is an Act that amended the *Criminal Code Act* (Ch. 262). Therefore, the offences as specified in that amending Act should be referred to as sections of the *Criminal Code* (Ch. 262), and not the *Criminal Code (Sexual Offences and Crimes Against Children) Act 2002*.

Although section 17 of the *Criminal Code (Sexual Offences and Crimes Against Children) Act 2002* states that section 347 of the Principal Act, ie., the *Criminal Code Act* (Ch. 262), is repealed its effect is to amend, rather than repeal.[346]

Section 347 of the *Criminal Code* (Ch. 262) was replaced with a section that enlarged its scope.

---

[345] See *The State v Kaupa Kokia* (2005) N3012, [2005] PGNC 16.

See also: *Attorney-General (Western Australia) v Marquet* (2003) 217 CLR 545; *Beaument v Yeomans* (1934) 3 SR (NSW) 562 at 569-570 and *Ex parte Todd* (1887) 19 QBD 186.

[346] See *The State v Dibol Petrus Kopal* (2004) N2778; *The State v Kaupa Kokia* (2005) N3012, [2005] PGNC 16 and *The State v Ludwick Jokar (No. 1)* (2008) N3361.

REPEALS

[1.0] INTRODUCTION

The meaning of the term 'repeal' is:

> to rescind the statute or statutory provision in question.[347]

A repealed law is to be treated as never having existed.[348]

A later statute may either:

- expressly, ie., as outlined in the statute in question[349];

  or

- impliedly, ie., by implication,

repeal another statute or sections of another statute.

Whether a statutory provision has been:

- amended[350];

  or

- repealed

is always a matter of substance, rather than the form of the provision.[351]

---

[347] See *Attorney-General (Western Australia) v Marquet* (2003) 217 CLR 545.

[348] See *Garo v The Police* [1985] PNGLR 320, [1985] PGSC 4.

[349] See section 63 of the *Interpretation Act* (Ch. 2).

See also: *Baiza Tadu Avona v The State* [1986] PNGLR 148 at 152, [1986] PGSC 2.

[350] The law in relation to the repeal of a statutory provision is also examined in the chapter titled 'Amendments'.

[351] See *Baiza Tadu Avona v The State* [1986] PNGLR 148 at 152, [1986] PGSC 2 and *The State v Kaupa Kokia* (2005) N3012, [2005] PGNC 16.

See also: *Attorney-General (Western Australia) v Marquet* (2003) 217 CLR 545 and *Beaument v Yeomans* (1934) 3 SR (NSW) 562 at 569-570.

REPEALS

The effect of the repeal of a statutory provision under which a substantive enactment has been made is generally to repeal the substantive enactment, unless the statute by which the repeal was effected discloses an intention to the contrary.[352]

[2.0] EXPRESSLY

[2.1] STATUTORY PROVISIONS

Section 63 of the *Interpretation Act* (Ch. 2) states:

> '(1) The repeal of a provision does not –
>
> (a) revive anything not in force or existing at the time at which the repeal takes effect; or
>
> (b) affect the previous operation of the repealed provision, or anything duly done or suffered under the repealed provision; or
>
> (c) affect any right, privilege, obligation, or liability acquired, accrued or incurred under the repealed provision[353]; or
>
> (d) affect any penalty, forfeiture, or punishment incurred in respect of an offence committed against the repealed provision; or
>
> (e) affect any investigation, legal proceeding or remedy in respect of any such right, privilege, obligation, liability, penalty, forfeiture or punishment,

---

[352] See *Bird v John Sharp and Sons Pty Ltd* (1942) 66 CLR 233 at 250; *Victorian Chamber of Manufacturers v The Commonwealth (Women's Employment Regulations)* (1943) 67 CLR 347 at 372 and *R v Kelly; ex parte Waterside Workers' Federation of Australia* (1952) 85 CLR 601 at 626-627.

See for example, the *Police Force Regulation* (Ch. 65). That regulation is continued under the *Police Act 1998*, notwithstanding that the *Police Force Act* (Ch. 65) has been repealed, see section 157(4) of the *Police Act 1998*.

[353] See *Joe Kua v John Wensti and Philip Kambu* (2004) N2772.

and any such investigation, legal proceeding, or remedy may be instituted, continued or enforced, and any such penalty, forfeiture, or punishment may be imposed, as if the repeal had not been made.[354]

(2) The repeal of a statutory provision that validated or continued in force any act, matter or thing does not affect the validation or continuance'.

Section 65 states:

'Where a statutory provision repeals another statutory provision and is to operate in place of the repealed provision, the repealed provision remains in force until the substituted provision comes into operation'.

Section 66 states:

'The repeal of a statutory provision by which another statutory provision was repealed does not, without express words, have the effect of reviving the last-mentioned provision'.

Section 67 states:

'The expiration of a statutory provision does not affect any civil or criminal proceeding previously commenced under the provision, but every such proceeding may be continued, and everything in relation to it be done, in all respects as if the provision continued in force'.

[354] As to the relationship between section 11 of the *Criminal Code* (Ch. 262) and this statutory provision, in relation to the *Criminal Code (Sexual Offences and Crimes Against Children) Act 2002*, see *Biaza Tadu Avona v State* [1986] PNGLR 148, [1986] PGSC 2; *Kape Sulu v The State* (2003) N2456; *The State v Tom Gaia and two others* (1986) N544; *The State v Moses Jafisa Winga (No. 1)* (2005) N2952, [2005] PGNC 168; *The State v Dibol Petrus Kopal* (2004) N2778; *The State v Thomas Angup* (2005) N2830; *The State v John Ritsi Kutetoa* (2005) N2814 and *The State v Ilam Peter* (2006) N3090.

REPEALS

[2.2] GENERAL PRINCIPLE

A law which has been repealed by statute, ie., expressly, is:

> to be treated as never having existed.[355]

An example of an Act that has been repealed is the *Police Force Act* (Ch. 65).[356]

[2.3] IMPLIEDLY

[2.3.1] INTRODUCTION

A statutory provision should be interpreted in such a way as to implement, rather than defeat, the legislative purpose by applying the rule 'ut magis quam pereat':

> it is better for a thing to have effect than to be made void.

There is no room for an implied repeal where there is an express provision to the effect that there shall not be any such an implied repeal.[357]

---

[355] See *SCR No. 4 of 1985; Omaro Garo v The Police* [1985] PNGLR 320, [1985] PGSC 4; *Gregory Ombalo v Sam Inguba – The Commissioner of Police and The Independent State of Papua New Guinea* (2004) N2725 and *The State v Thomas Angup* (2005) N2830.

See also: *Kay v Goodwin* (1830) 6 Bing 576; *Lemm v Mitchell* [1912] AC 400; *Surtees v Ellison* (1829) 9 B & C 750; *Bennett v Tatton* (1918) 88 LJKB 313; *R v Inhabitants of Mawgan* (1838) 8 Ad & El 496; *R v Inhabitants of Denton* (1852) 18 QB 761; *R v McKenzie* (1820) Russ & Ry 429 and *R v Swan* (1849) 4 Cox CC 108.

[356] See section 157(1) of the *Police Act 1998*.

[357] See *R v Gover* (2000) 118 A Crim R 8.

[3.2] DIFFERENT STATUTES

Where the later of two statutes makes a provision that is inconsistent with an earlier statute, the latter is:

> to be taken to have impliedly repealed the former.[358]

This rule, however, does not apply where:

- the prior statute is special;

  and

- the subsequent statute general.[359]

In such a case the Court applies the rule 'generalis specialibus non derogant'.[360]

The test to be applied as to whether there has been such an implied repeal is as follows:

> Are the provisions of the later statute so inconsistent with, or repugnant to, the provisions of the earlier statute that the two cannot stand together?[361]

---

[358] See *The State v Natpalau Tulong* [1995] PNGLR 329 at 331 and *The State v Kiap Bonga* [1988-89] PNGLR 360, [1989] PGNC 125.

See also: *Dr Foster's Case* (1614) 11 Co Rep 56b; 77 ER 1222; *Garnett v Bradley* (1878) 3 App Cas 944 at 966 and *Rose v Hvric* (1963) 108 CLR 353, (1963) 37 ALJR 1 at 3.

[359] See *McGonagle v McGonagle* [1951] IR 123.

[360] See *McGonagle v McGonagle* [1951] IR 123.

[361] See *Churchwardens and Overseers of West Ham v Fourth City Mutual Building Society* [1892] 1 QB 654 at 658.

Other tests have included whether it was intended that one statute should stand in place of another [see *Mitchell v Scales* (1907) 5 CLR 405, per Isaacs J at 417] and whether effect can be given to both statutes at the same time [see *Rose v Hvric* (1963) 108 CLR 353 at 360, (1963) 37 ALJR 1].

If however both statutes can reasonably be interpreted in such a way that both can be given effect to, then this must be done.[362]

In the absence of express words, an earlier statutory provision is not repealed, altered or derogated from by a later provision, unless an intention to that effect is necessarily to be implied.[363]

Furthermore, if a later statute contains a list of statutes that it expressly repeals then an omission of a particular statute from that list provides an indication that it is unlikely that it intended to repeal that earlier statute.[364]

However, the more detailed and elaborate the later statute the more probable it is that it will be interpreted to have impliedly repealed the earlier statute.[365]

If statutory provisions are not wholly inconsistent then to the extent of the consistency there would be an implied repeal.[366]

[3.3] SAME STATUTE

Inconsistency within the same statute is rare, but not unknown.[367]

---

[362] See *The State v Natpalau Tulong* [1995] PNGLR 329 at 331; *Laho Kerekere v Robin Miria* [1983] PNGLR 277 at 280 and *Hedura Transport Pty Ltd v Gairo Vegoli* (1977) N99.

See also: *Sweeney v Fitzhardinge* (1906) 4 CLR 716 at 726, [1906] HCA 73; *R v Wheeldon* (1978) 18 ALR 619 at 622, (1978) 33 FLR 402 at 405-406, [1978] FCA 11; *Commissioner of Stamp Duties v Permanent Trustee Co Ltd* (1987) 9 NSWLR 719 at 722-724; *Le Blanc v Queensland TAB Ltd* [2003] 2 Qd R 65, [2002] QSC 323; *Southside Autos (1981) Pty Ltd v Commissioner of State Revenue* (2008) 37 WAR 245, [2008] WASCA 208 and *Trajkoski v Director of Public Prosecutions (Western Australia)* [2010] WASCA 119.

[363] See *Re Chance* [1936] Ch 266 and *Seward v The Vera Cruz* (1884) 10 App Cas 59, per Lord Selborne at 68.

See also: *Saraswati v R* (1991) 172 CLR 1, per Gaudron J at 17-18, [1991] HCA 21; *Auckland Gas Co v Auckland City Council* [1990] 2 NZLR 420, per Somers J at 425 and *R v Teina Pora* [2000] NZCA 233.

[364] See *The State v Natpalau Tulong* [1995] PNGLR 329 at 331.

[365] See *Jennings Industries Ltd v Commonwealth* (1984) 57 ACTR 5 at 21.

[366] See *Goodwin v Phillips* (1908) 7 CLR 1, per Griffith CJ at 7.

[367] See *R v Teina Pora* [2000] NZCA 233.

REPEALS

There was a rule of statutory interpretation that where there is an irreconcilable inconsistency between two statutory provisions in the same statute, the latter must prevail, even though it may be considered to be a rule of last resort.[368]

Such a rule of statutory interpretation is no longer considered appropriate and is considered inconsistent with the purposive rule of statutory interpretation.[369]

In such circumstances the current rule is:

> the Court is to decide whether the statutory provisions can be reconciled

because an interpretation that enables the provisions to work together is preferred.[370]

Reconciling conflicting provisions will often require the Court to:

- determine which is the leading provision;

  and

- determine which is the subordinate provision,

and therefore which is to be considered rendered ineffective to the extent of the inconsistency.[371]

---

[368] See *Re Williams* (1887) 36 Ch D 573 at 578; *Dobbs v Grand Junction Waterworks Co* (1883) 9 App Cases 49 and *Ellen Street Estates Ltd v Minister of Health* [1934] 1 KB 590.

See also: *Goodwin v Phillips* (1908) 7 CLR 1 at 7; *South Eastern Drainage Board (South Australia) v Savings Bank of South Australia* (1939) 62 CLR 603 and *R v Teina Pora* [2000] NZCA 233.

[369] See *Re Marr and another (bankrupts)* [1990] 2 All ER 880, [1990] Ch 773, per Nicholls LJ at 784-785; *Wybrow v Chief Electoral Officer* [1980] 1 NZLR 147 and *R v Moore* [1995] 4 All ER 843.

[370] See *Hedura Transport Pty Ltd v Gairo Vegoli* (1977) N99.

See also: *Institute of Patent Agents v Lockwood* [1894] AC 347, per Herschell LC at 360; *Re Marr and another (bankrupts)* [1990] 2 All ER 880, [1990] Ch 773, per Nicholls LJ at 784-785; *R v Teina Pora* [2000] NZCA 233 and *Butler v Attorney-General (Victoria)* (1961) 106 CLR 268, per Fullagar J at 276 and Windeyer J at 290.

[371] See *Institute of Patent Agents v Lockwood* [1894] AC 347, per Herschell LC at 360.

See also: *Re Marr and another (bankrupts)* [1990] 2 All ER 880, [1990] Ch 773, per Nicholls LJ at 784-785 and *R v Teina Pora* [2000] NZCA 233.

The conflict must be alleviated, so far as possible[372], by interpreting the meaning of the competing provisions to achieve that result that will best give effect to the purpose and language of those provisions while maintaining the unity of all the provisions.[373]

When there are two possible interpretations of a statutory provision and one is reasonable and the other is less reasonable or leads to an absurdity then a Court should adopt a more reasonable interpretation.[374]

It is proper for a Court to adopt the interpretation that will avoid consequences that appear to be irrational and unjust.[375]

---

[372] However, such an interpretation may not be possible, see *South-Eastern Drainage Board (South Australia) v Savings Bank of South Australia* (1939) 62 CLR 603, per Dixon J at 626-627.

[373] See *Australian Alliance Assurance Co Ltd v Attorney-General (Queensland)* [1916] St R Qd 135, per Cooper CJ at 161 and *Minister for Resources v Dover Fisheries Pty Ltd* (1993) 43 FCR 565, per Gummow J at 574.

[374] See *New Britain Oil Palm Ltd and others v Vitus Sukuramu* (2008) SC946, [2008] PGSC 29.

See also: *Caledonian Railway Co v North British Railway Co* (1881) 6 App Cases 114.

[375] See *Soso Tumu for Luhalipu Clan and others v Independent State of Papua New Guinea and others* (2002) N2190.

See also: *Public Transport Commission of New South Wales v J Murray-More (New South Wales) Pty Ltd* (1975) 6 ALR 271, per Gibbs J at 282.

SUBORDINATE LEGISLATIVE ENACTMENTS

[1.0] CONSTITUTIONAL PROVISIONS

Section 10 of the *Constitution of the Independent State of Papua New Guinea* states (in part):

'All written laws (other than this Constitution) shall be read and construed subject to –

(c) in the case of adopted laws or subordinate legislative enactments -- the organic laws and the laws by or under which they were enacted or made, and so as not to exceed the authority to make them properly given, to the intent that where any such law would, but for this section, have been in excess to the authority so given it shall nevertheless be a valid law to the extent to which it is not in excess of that authority'.

Section 116(1) states:

'All subordinate legislative enactments[376] made under an Act of the Parliament –

(a) shall be tabled in the Parliament as soon as practicable, and in any event within seven sitting days of the Parliament, after being made; and

(b) are subject to disallowance in whole or in part by decision of the Parliament,

in accordance with Section Sch.1.18 (*disallowance, etc.*) and the Standing Orders of the Parliament'.

[2.0] INTERPRETATION ACT[377]

Section 3 of the *Interpretation Act* (Ch. 2) defines the term 'regulation' as meaning:

'a regulation made under an Act, and includes rules and by-laws so made'.

Section 73 states:

'A reference in an Act --

(a) to a regulation, without further identification, is a reference to a regulation made under that Act; and

---

376 The term 'subordinate legislative enactment' is defined in Schedule 1.2.2 of the *Constitution of the Independent State of Papua New Guinea* as meaning 'a regulation or any other instrument (whether of a legislative nature or not) made under a statute'.

Referred to as 'Legislative Instruments' in the *Interpretation Act* (Ch. 2), see the definition of the term 'subordinate legislative enactment' in section 3(1) of that Act.

377 Refer also to the other provisions of Part IV of the *Interpretation Act* (Ch. 2).

(b) to "the regulation" is a reference to any regulations made under this Act'.

For example:

Section 47 of the *Motor Traffic Act* (Ch. 243) states:

- 'The Head of State, acting on advice, may make regulations, not inconsistent with this Act; prescribing all matters under this Act are required or permitted to be prescribed, or that are necessary or convenient to be prescribed for carrying out or giving effect to this Act [...]';

  and

- the *Motor Traffic Regulation* (Ch. 243) states that it is 'Made under the Motor Traffic Act'.

[3.0] GENERAL PRINCIPLES[378]

When an Act of Parliament authorises an 'authority' to make subordinate legislative enactments then the 'authority' must:

act within the powers given to it.[379]

---

[378] Refer also to the section titled 'Extrinsic Aids' in the chapter titled 'Aids To Interpretation'.

See also: *Chambers v Mayos* [1969-70] PNGLR 46 and *Casper Wallace v Ron Napitalai for and on behalf of the Board Appeal Committee of PNG Ports Corporation Limited and PNG Ports Corporation Limited* (2008) N3431.

[379] See *NTN Pty Limited and NBN Limited v The State* [1986] PNGLR 167 at 178 and *SCR No. 5 of 1987; Central Banking (Foreign Exchange and Gold) Regulations (Ch. 138)* [1987] PNGLR 433, [1987] PGSC 4.

Unreasonableness is an *ultra vires* (ie., beyond power) ground of judicial review of delegated legislation; its essence being that the authority delegated the law-making power has gone beyond the limits of its power, see *Matu Mining Pty Ltd v Philemon Embel (Attorney-General) and Kare Puga Development Corporation Pty Ltd*; *Telepage Pty Ltd v PTC* (1987) N605; *NTN Pty Ltd and NBN Ltd v The State* [1986] PNGLR 167; *Pansat Communication Pty Ltd v John Momis and others* (1995) N1321; *Hanjung Power Limited v Dr Allan Marat, Attorney-General and others* (2009) N3751 and *Kuya Keli v Theodore Kelu* [1978] PNGLR 217.

See also: *Irving v Aske* [1870] LR 5 QB 208.

If the 'authority' goes beyond those powers then it exercises powers that are not given to it by the relevant statute or Parliament.[380]

Whilst allowing for the difference in juridical nature and provenance, a subordinate legislative enactment is to be interpreted in the same way as an Act.[381]

A subordinate legislative enactment must be interpreted according to the statute under which it was made, ie., the enabling statute.[382]

---

[380] See *NTN Pty Limited and NBN Limited v The State* [1986] PNGLR 167 at 178 and *SCR No. 5 of 1987; Central Banking (Foreign Exchange and Gold) Regulations (Ch. 138)* [1987] PNGLR 433, [1987] PGSC 4.

Unreasonableness is an *ultra vires* (ie., beyond power) ground of judicial review of delegated legislation; its essence being that the authority delegated the law-making power has gone beyond the limits of its power, see *Matu Mining Pty Ltd v Philemon Embel (Attorney-General) and Kare Puga Development Corporation Pty Ltd*; *Telepage Pty Ltd v PTC* (1987) N605; *NTN Pty Ltd and NBN Ltd v The State* [1986] PNGLR 167; *Pansat Communication Pty Ltd v John Momis and others* (1995) N1321; *Hanjung Power Limited v Dr Allan Marat, Attorney-General and others* (2009) N3751 and *Kuya Keli v Theodore Kelu* [1978] PNGLR 217.

See also: *Irving v Aske* [1870] LR 5 QB 208.

381 See Bennion, 'Statutory Interpretation - A Code', 3rd ed., 1997, page 190.

See also: section 77 of the *Interpretation Act* (Ch. 2).

[382] See section 10(c) of the *Constitution of the Independent State of Papua New Guinea.*

See also: *Reference pursuant to Constitution Section 18(2) concerning interpretation and application of section 193(1A) and (1C) Constitution to section 31A and 31C of the Public Services (Management) Act and Reservation pursuant to section 15 of the Supreme Court Act (Ch 37); Re O.S. No. 241 of 2008 (JR) and The Matter of an Application for Judicial Review under Order 16 of the National Court Rules; Isaac Lupari v Sir Michael Somare, MP – Prime Minister and Chairman of the National Executive Council and the Independent State of Papua New Guinea* (2008) SC930, [2008] PGSC 19; *Matu Mining Pty Ltd v Philemon Embel (Attorney-General) and Kare Puga Development Corporation Pty Ltd* (1995) SC483; *NTN Pty Ltd and NBN Ltd v The State* [1986] PNGLR 167, per Kidu CJ at 178 and *Pansat Communication Pty Ltd v John Momis and others* (1995) N1321.

See for example, section 47 of the *Motor Traffic Act* (Ch. 243) and the *Motor Traffic Regulation* (Ch. 243).

GENDER AND NUMBER

Section 6 of the *Interpretation Act* (Ch. 2) states:

'In a statutory provision –

(a) words importing the masculine gender include females; and

(b) words in the singular include the plural and words in the plural include the singular[383]'.

[383] Such a provision assists to avoid cumbersome and over-elaborate wording in statutes, see *Blue Metal Industries Ltd v R W Diley* [1970] AC 827, per Lord Morris.

RETROSPECTIVITY

Legislation may have a retrospective effect, ie., apply to the past.[384]

However, there is a presumption against retrospectivity.

But this presumption may be removed by Parliament by express provision in a statute.[385]

A statute is retrospective if it:

- takes away a vested right acquired under an existing law;
- impairs a vested right acquired under an existing law;
- creates a new obligation;
- imposes a new duty;

  or

- attaches a new disability

in regard to events already past.[386]

No statute should be interpreted so as to have a retrospective effect, unless its language is such as plainly to require such an interpretation.[387]

---

[384] See section 110 of the *Constitution of the Independent State of Papua New Guinea* and section 66(3)(b) of the *Constitution of the Autonomous Region of Bougainville*.

[385] See section 110(2)(b) of the *Constitution of the Independent State of Papua New Guinea* and section 66(3)(b) of the *Constitution of the Autonomous Region of Bougainville*.

[386] See *The Director – Division of District Administration and others v The Sacred Heart Mission (New Britain) Property Trust* [1974] PNGLR 312.

See also: *Yew Bon Tew v Kenderaan Bas Mara* [1983] 1 AC 553, per Lord Brightman at 558-559; *Marshal v Apong* [1998] 1 WLR 674, per Lord Slynn at 678; *R v JS* [2007] NSWCCA 272; *Reid v Reid* (1886) 31 Ch D 402; *Lauri v Renad* [1892] 3 Ch 402 and *Attorney-General (New South Wales) v World Best Holdings Ltd* (2005) 63 NSWLR 557, [2005] NSWCA 261.

[387] See *The Director – Division of District Administration and others v The Sacred Heart Mission (New Britain) Property Trust* [1974] PNGLR 312.

See also: *Turnbull v Forman* (1885) 15 QBD 234, per Bowen LJ at 238; *Reid v Reid* (1886) 31 Ch D 402, per Bowen LJ at 408-409; *Lauri v Renad* [1892] 3 Ch 402, per Lindley LJ at 420-421; *Singer v R* [1932] SCR 70 and *Boyer v R* [1949] SCR 89.

RETROSPECTIVITY

Penal legislation is ordinarily not to be given retrospective effect.[388]

As stated by the Supreme Court in *Polem Enterprise Ltd v Attorney-General of Papua New Guinea, Mr. Francis Damem and others*[389]:

> 'Individuals and corporations conduct their affairs, business and daily lives according to the law as it exists from time to time. That is the essence of the Rule of Law. It is why there is a presumption against retrospectivity in the application of all sorts of laws. Applying laws retrospectively is akin to changing the rules of a game of football after the game has finished and then applying the new rules to see who won. That is why it is done sparingly, only in exceptional cases'.

As a general rule:

> a statute is prima facie construed as not attaching new legal consequences to facts and events that occurred before its commencement.[390]

There is a presumption against a statute having retrospective operation, unless such an interpretation:

- appears very clearly in the terms of the statute[391];

  or

---

388 See *Waddington v Miah* [1974] 59 Cr App R 149, per Lord Reid at 150-151.

389 (2007) SC911, [2008] PGSC 9.

390 See *Fisher v Hebburn Ltd* (1960) 105 CLR 188 at 194, [1960] HCA 80; *Mathieson v Burton* (1971) 124 CLR 1 at 22, [1971] HCA 4 and *Geraldton Building Co Pty Ltd v May* (1977) 136 CLR 379, per Stephen J at 399-400 and Mason J at 401, [1977] HCA 17.

391 See *The State v Tom Gaia and two others* (1986) N544; *Custodian of Expropriated Property and Phoebe Kroening v Commissioner of Native Affairs (Re Mortlock Islands)* [1971-72] PNGLR 621 and *Soso Tumu for Luhalipu Clan and others v Independent State of Papua New Guinea and others* (2002) N2190.

See also: *Maxwell v Murphy* (1957) 96 CLR 261 at 267, [1957] HCA 7; *Rodway v R* (1990) 169 CLR 515, [1990] HCA 19; *Newell v R* (1936) 55 CLR 707; *Daniels Corporation International Pty Ltd v Australian Competition and Consumer Commission* (2002) 213 CLR 543; *Plaintiff S157/2002 v The Commonwealth* (2003) 211 CLR 476; *Al-Kateb v Godwin* (2004) 219 CLR 562; *Fisher v Hebburn Ltd* (1960) 105 CLR 188, [1960] HCA 80; *Attorney-General (Western Australia) v Marquet* (2003) 217 CLR 545; *Young v Adams* [1898] AC 469; *R v JS* [2007] NSWCCA 272; *R v Secretary of State to the Home Department; ex parte Pierson* [1998] AC 539; *R v Secretary of State for the Home Department; ex parte Simms* [2002] 2 AC 115 and *Richardson v Brennan* [1966] WAR 159, per Wolff CJ at 160.

- arises by necessary and distinct application[392].

But that presumption has no application to statutory provisions that affect only procedure[393] and practice.[394]

However, a classification of a statute that it is procedural or substantive does not necessarily determine whether the statute may have a retrospective operation.[395]

Indeed, strictly speaking where procedure alone is involved, a statute will invariably operate prospectively because it will prescribe the manner in which something may or must be done in the future, even if what is to be done relates to, or is based upon past events.[396]

---

[392] See *Cardshops Limited v John Lewis Properties Limited* [1982] 3 All ER 746 at 756.

[393] See *Re Athlumney; ex parte Wilson* [1898] 2 QB 547, per Wright J at 551.

See also: *R v Makanjuola* [1995] 3 All ER 730, (1995) 2 Cr App R 469, per Taylor LCJ at 472; *Mathieson v Burton* (1971) 124 CLR 1 at 32, [1971] HCA 4; *Carr v Finance Corporation of Australia Ltd* (1982) 56 ALJR 730 at 738; *Maxwell v Murphy* (1957) 96 CLR 261, [1957] HCA 7; *Victrawl Pty Ltd v Telstra Corporation Ltd* (1995) 183 CLR 595 at 615, [1995] HCA 51; *Rodway v R* (1990) 169 CLR 515 at 518, [1990] HCA 19; *McKain v R W Miller and Co (South Australia) Pty Ltd* (1991) 174 CLR 1 at 26-27, [1991] HCA 56; *John Pfeiffer Pty Ltd v Rogerson* (2000) 203 CLR 503, [2000] HCA 36 and *R v Le Sarge* 26 CCC (2d) 388, per Houlden J.

[394] See *Milne Bay Provincial Government v The Honorable Roy Evara MP Minister for Primary Industry and The Independent State of Papua New Guinea* [1981] PNGLR 63, per Andrew J at 66.

[395] See *Rodway v R* (1990) 169 CLR 515 at 519, [1990] HCA 19.

[396] See *R v Lujanage* [1966] 1 All ER 650 at 659.

See also: *R v Makanjuola* [1995] 3 All ER 730, (1995) 2 Cr App R 469; *Rodway v R* (1990) 169 CLR 515, [1990] HCA 19; *Nicholas v R* [1998] FJCA 9 and *R v Christian (No. 2)* [2005] LRC 745, [2005] PNSC 1.

RETROSPECTIVITY

A person who commits an offence does not have a right to be tried in any particular way; merely a right to be tried according to the practice and procedure prevailing at the time of trial.[397]

There is a well-established distinction between a true statute of limitations, which operates to bar a right of action independently existing, but does not extinguish that right, on the one hand, and a limitation period annexed by a statute to a right which it creates, on the other.[398] A true statute of limitations has been classified as procedural in nature. By contrast, a limitation period which creates a right of limited duration so that, after the expiry of the prescribed time, the right ceases to exist for any purpose, has been classified as substantive in nature.[399]

---

[397] See *Wright v Hale* (1860) 6 H & N 227, 158 ER 94, per Wilde B at 233 and 96; *Attorney-General v Sillem* (1864) 10 HLC 704, 11 ER 1200, per Lord Wensleydale at 763 and 1224 and *Warner v Murdoch* (1877) 4 ChD 750, per James LJ at 752.

See also: *Maxwell v Murphy* (1957) 96 CLR 261 at 267, [1957] HCA 7 and *Rodway v R* (1990) 169 CLR 515 at 521, [1990] HCA 19.

As regards proceedings that are pending, see *Re Joseph Suche and Co Ltd* [1875] 1 ChD 48 at 50; *Hutchinson v Jauncey* [1950] 1 KB 574 at 579; *Continental Liqueurs Pty Ltd v G F Heublein and Bro Inc* (1960) 103 CLR 422 at 427; *Zainal bin Hashim v Government of Malaysia* [1980] AC 734 at 742; *L'Office Cherifien Des Phosphates v Yamashita-Shinnihon Steamship Co Ltd* [1994] 1 AC 496 at 495-495 and 524-525; *Wilson v First County Trust Ltd (No. 2)* [2004] 1 AC 816; *State of Victoria v Robertson* [2000] 1 VR 465 and *Attorney-General (New South Wales) v World Best Holdings Ltd* (2005) 63 NSWLR 557, [2005] NSWCA 261.

[398] See *Australian Iron and Steel Ltd v Hoogland* (1962) 108 CLR 471, per Windeyer J at 488, [1962] HCA 13 and *Commonwealth v Verwayen* (1990) 170 CLR 394, per McHugh J at 497, [1990] HCA 39.

As regards amendments to statutory limitation provisions for the commencement of legal proceedings, see *Rodway v R* (1990) 169 CLR 515 at 519, [1990] HCA 19.

[399] See *McKain v R W Miller and Co (South Australia) Pty Ltd* (1992) 174 CLR 1 at 43-44, [1991] HCA 56.

COMPUTATION OF TIME AND DISTANCE

[1.0] TIME

Section 11 of the *Interpretation Act* (Ch. 2) states:

'(1) In computing time for the purposes of a statutory provision, a period of time from –

(a) a certain day; or

(b) the happening of an event; or

(c) the doing of an act or thing,

shall be deemed to be exclusive of the certain day or of the day on which the event happens or the act or thing is done.

(2) If the last day of a period prescribed or allowed by a statutory provision for the doing of an act falls on a Sunday or a public holiday, the act may be done on the day next following that is not a Sunday or public holiday.

(3) Where a statutory provision directs or allows an act or proceeding to be done or taken on a certain day, then if that day happens to be a Sunday or public holiday the act or proceeding shall be considered as done or taken in due time if it is done or taken on the day next following that is not a Sunday or public holiday.

(4) Where a statutory provision directs or allows an act or proceeding to be done or taken within a time not exceeding eight days, Sundays and public holidays shall not be taken into account in the computation of the time'.

Section 12 states:

'Where no time is prescribed or allowed within which an act is required or permitted by a statutory provision to be done, the act shall or may be done, as the case may be, with all convenient speed and as often as the occasion arises'.

[2.0] DISTANCE

Section 13 of the *Interpretation Act* (Ch. 2) states:

'In the measurement of a distance for the purposes of a statutory provision, the distance shall be measured in a straight line on a horizontal plane'.

INDEX

INDEX

Page

INDEX

INDEX

www.ingramcontent.com/pod-product-compliance
Lightning Source LLC
LaVergne TN
LVHW062149200926
848484LV00007B/1892